How To Choose, Operate and Market Your Home-Based Business

Practical Advice for Operating a Small Business on a Shoestring Budget

By Susan E. Barton

The Write Words 4 You
eBook Review Gal
About.me/ebookreviewgal

Susan Barton's previous book, *How To Write, Publish and Market Your eBook*, is available on Amazon and other online book sellers.

"You cannot plough a field by turning it over in your mind."

~ Anonymous

Foreword

As a single mother, who raised three wonderful (most of the time) children, I did more than my fair share of juggling several home-based businesses in order to support the four of us. Well, not usually several businesses at once, but quite often it felt that way. After all, motherhood is a full-time job on its own. Where did I get the nerve to think I could pile on one or two more jobs? It was mainly out of necessity, although I'll be the first to admit to this day my hyperactive personality won't allow me to sit idle for any length of time.

From freelance receptionist in my twenties, to now author and book marketer I realize I've been pretty darn busy over the years. I've gained a ton of valuable information along the way and I'm always willing to help other entrepreneurs achieve their own, individual goals. Hence, the reason for this book.

I know how difficult it is to make ends meet on two salaries, let alone on only one. There are many people, stay at home moms in particular, who could use a part-time income to help with the bills. I wanted to share my knowledge. I wanted to show that ANYONE could choose, operate and market a business. Lastly, I wanted to prove it could be done with little to no start-up costs, enabling you to make money today and not six months from now. Additionally, I chose small businesses that required either very little training and/or certification - most of these ideas require no training or certification at all. How great is that?!

At a time when college grads are entering the workforce with thousands of dollars in student loan debt hanging over their heads, there are still dozens of ways to make a very comfortable part-time or full-time income. Looking at things from a creative perspective is all it takes to get started. I've attempted to light the spark of an idea in your mind. Take these ideas, make them your own and run with them. I wish you great success in all you do!

Sincerely,

Susan Barton

If you'd like to get in touch with me to let me know what you think, or if you'd like to share your entrepreneurial story with me I would love to hear from you! You might even end up in my next book! Please contact me via: info@thewritewords4you.com.

Contents

Introduction

How many times have you come home from work after a long day and thought, *there has to be a better way to earn a living*? Far too many employers have adopted a less than understanding and caring attitude towards their hardworking employees. They know if they lose an employee there are dozens of other candidates waiting right behind them.

Although the term "in this economy" is often overused, it certainly indicates the current sentiment of many consumers. Things are tough. Families are finding it harder than ever to make ends meet - even families with more than one income. Compound this with the ever-changing unemployment rate and we realize that many people are just one paycheck away from financial disaster.

At the time of this writing, the current national unemployment rate is 6.7%. Obviously, that figure is quite high. In addition, those Americans who are employed have found themselves with drastically reduced work hours. Whether it's due to corporate greed, or actual profit loss, many major corporations have downgraded full-time employees to merely part-time. Few Americans can pay their bills on a part-time salary.

It's not all doom and gloom, however. We, as a nation, are resilient, determined and inventive individuals. *No jobs? No problem. I'll create my own!* Many Americans recognize that starting a business is a viable, practical response to the current unemployment situation in our country. Millions of small businesses are started each year in our country. Some fail, while others thrive. A lot goes into starting a business. Proper planning is essential - particularly if you intend to seek financial backing. A great deal of work goes into starting and running a business too. Most small business owners report underestimating the time and effort involved. But, the fact that taking the entrepreneurial plunge is a feasible option for just about anyone is exciting and encouraging.

A down economy isn't the only reason why so many people start their own businesses. Independence, freedom, individuality and a desire to ditch the daily 9 to 5 grind are often first and foremost for many people. We've all been there - stuck in a dead-end job, with no foreseeable future. It can be downright depressing. How great would it be to wake up every morning, commute to your living room and be in charge of your own day?

Stay at home moms (SAHMs) understand the importance of squeezing every last penny out of a household budget. It's difficult supporting a family on a single income, but raising small children at home, rather than sending them off to an expensive daycare, is often a priority. A part-time, home based business can boost the family finances in ways many moms never thought possible.

This book provides a wealth of information, gathered from personal experience, as well as from meticulous research. The information provided here will help you assess your skills, choose a business and perform daily operations and marketing. *How To Choose, Operate and Market Your Home-Based Business* shares tips, tricks and techniques for reaching your own individual goals of entrepreneurship!

First Things First

You may already have an idea of the type of business you'd like to start. On the other hand, maybe you don't have a clue. You just know you have a burning desire to be your own boss, in charge of your own hours and professional creativity. Either way, you'll want to do your homework before progressing any further. You should ask yourself a few questions before proceeding:

Do I want to Sell Products or Services?

Selling products usually, but not always, requires maintaining a steady supply of inventory. Ask yourself:

- Do I have room to store products?
- Do I have the cash to purchase inventory?
- Will the need to ship products quickly become a burden? (This requires purchasing packaging materials, frequent trips to the post office, dealing with lost, damaged or delayed shipments, etc.)
- Will the shelf life of my product dictate storage, production and shipping requirements?

Service businesses are not without their own specific issues, but they're often less expensive and easier to start because:

- There are usually no storage requirements.
- Production is usually minimal or non-existent.
- There are no associated shipping costs.

What Are My *Soft* Skills?

Whether you wish to start a product or service related business, you should be as honest as possible with yourself when deciding the following. Begin by assessing your *soft skills*:

- Am I a people-person? If not, you'd better brush up on your customer service skills asap or you'll soon find yourself unhappy and without customers. It takes a great deal of patience, tolerance and diplomacy to work directly with consumers. If you don't possess these skills yourself all is not lost, you could consider hiring a *front man* for this purpose.

- How accommodating will I be with my clients and customers? Am I prepared to go above and beyond the typical business owner/client relationship? Without a doubt, you will eventually run across an unhappy customer. Are you willing to do whatever it takes to keep him or her satisfied, even if it means you'll lose money on a job?

- Am I a team player? Your business won't operate in a vacuum. Not only will you deal on a daily basis with clients, you'll interact with suppliers, other contractors, wholesalers and others. You'll need to remain flexible when it comes to shipping times, meetings, etc.

- How good are you at delegating responsibilities? There might come a time when you'll need to hire employees. If you're not comfortable handing over some of the minor tasks to your subordinates you'll end up running yourself ragged in no time.

- Are you willing and able to eventually train someone else? Not everyone has the skill to train people properly. You might know exactly what needs to be done and how to do it, but you will end up frustrated if you don't correctly train your employees.

- How organized are you? You will need to keep meticulous records of business expenses, shipping, receiving, billing, inventory, etc. If you're disorganized you'll find yourself missing ordering deadlines, without inventory and allowing balances to remain unpaid.

- Do you have a tendency to be indecisive, inflexible or rigid? Indecisiveness has no place in business operations. You will often need to make quick decisions and then learn to stick with them. Being seen as wishy-washy can easily become a liability in business. On the flip side, stubbornness will result in the loss of customers. Accommodating the needs of your clients is part of good customer service and is essential if you wish your business to succeed. Walking a fine line and practicing a certain amount of business finesse is crucial to the growth of your small business.

- Are you (and your family) prepared for the long hours that are necessary to run a home based business? Almost every small business owner reports working more hours than they ever did while working for someone else. Chances are you'll be working well into the evening and on weekends. Will your family be accepting of this?

If you've identified any of the above questions as being problematic you'll want to think long and hard about starting your own business. You'll find that, while you won't be able to change the attitude of customers, suppliers and others, you can most certainly change your own.

What Are My *Hard* Skills?

Next, you'll want to assess your *hard skills*. These are your tangible skills, such as computer knowledge, typing skills and other areas of expertise. To decide what these are you should make a list that includes:

- Past and present employment. Break each job down into duty requirements.

- Any certifications you hold, seminars or other training sessions you've attended.
- Volunteer work. List any organizations you may have assisted and what services you provided. Just because you didn't get paid for keeping your church's books, organizing PTA functions or creating club flyers, doesn't mean these things haven't added to your work experience.
- Hobbies and past-times. Proficiency in a hobby can easily translate into a small business.

Small Business Ideas

Once you have your hard and soft skills list, you should have a good idea where your strengths, skills and expertise lie. Now it's time to make a list of possible businesses. Several business ideas have been broken down into categories and discussed on the following pages. Some of these ideas are ordinary and utilitarian, and others are unique and niche-specific. Filling a niche can result in the operation of a popular business - the *"now, why didn't I think of that?!"* phenomenon, so to speak.

Almost all of these small business ideas require absolutely no certification or specialized training, so you can get started right away. Additionally, many do not require any start-up capital. These are businesses that practically anyone can start, regardless of educational background or financial situation. However, as a business owner you should never stop learning and improving the way you do business. Keeping updated in a specific field or industry shows customers that you provide only the most up-to-date products and services.

Take any of these ideas and put your own spin on it. Geographical location definitely dictates how quickly a business will take off and flourish. The larger the city, the more potential clients you'll be able to reach. But that doesn't mean you should shy away from a business because you're located in a rural, less populated area. It just means you'll have to adjust the way you operate, advertise and find customers. Choose a business you'll be passionate about and good things will follow!

Craft & Hobby

Your creativity, artistic abilities and unique imagination can serve you well in creating a business. The internet is filled with sites selling handmade and artistic items. Whether you knit, crochet, paint original art, create jewelry, sew, etc., there's a market for your handiwork. This is an excellent part-time or full-time business for stay at home moms. Crafting products to sell while little ones are napping can result in a sizeable inventory of products.

Purchase your supplies from wholesalers whenever possible. This keeps production costs down, and allows you to raise your profits and pass the savings on to customers. Search online for wholesalers specializing in the products you'll be using most often. You might have to register for a resale certificate through your state, as most wholesalers require this. The potential savings are definitely worth the effort. You'll likely need to do this when preparing your taxes anyway, so you may as well do it from the start.

If you find you can't meet the wholesale seller's minimum purchase, consider pooling your order with friends, family and other crafters. This is a great way for everyone to save money. Many wholesalers require an initial order of $150 or more. If you don't have friends or family interested in a co-op arrangement, you can make some money back by selling craft supplies to your crafty friends or even your customers. You can make a nice income simply selling craft supplies you've purchased via online wholesalers.

The following are some ideas for selling your handmade items.

Arts & Crafts Websites

Joining an online market and selling your handcrafted items is simple, quick and affordable. Registration is almost always free. There are almost always listing and final sales fees involved. Although, *Shop Handmade*, similar to *Etsy*, does not charge any fees at the time of this writing.

Most sites allow users to set up an online shop, complete with shop banner, bio, description and profile picture. Make the most of these features to set your shop apart from all the rest. Take clear, clutter-free and colorful photos of your items and use one or two in your banner. Potential customers will admire these photos and want to know more about your shop.

Consider registering an online shop with the following sellers:

- *Etsy*
- *Shop Handmade* (like Etsy, but FREE)
- *Uncommon Goods*
- *DaWanda*
- *Bonanza*
- *Artfire*
- *Made it Myself*
- *iCraft*
- *Silkfair*

*If you're in the UK, consider selling on *Folksy*, since only UK-based sellers are permitted.

Your Own Website

It's quick and easy to purchase a domain name, find a hosting site and start selling your handcrafted items via your own website. You can accept payments via PayPal directly on your site. This increases your profits since you won't be paying any listing or final sales fees to an online marketplace. However, PayPal does charge sellers a small processing fee.

You may wish to experiment with a free website at first. WordPress.com and Blogger are the two biggies. However, while Blogger enables users to paste a PayPal button code into posts, WordPress.com does not. If you opt for a WordPress.com website you will have to come up with an alternate payment method.

Choose a website template that is photo-friendly and specifically designed for highlighting individual items. Great photos sell items more quickly. There are many photography-style templates available via WordPress and Blogger. You want to make it as simple as possible to add and remove product photos as your items are added and sold.

Craft Shows and Flea Markets

This option is definitely not for everyone. A great deal of work goes into setting up and tearing down craft booths. There is also a fair amount of travel involved, making it necessary to find a safe, secure way of transporting your products to the various craft shows and flea markets. You may wish to participate only in local fairs and markets, but there are many extremely popular venues across the country that make travel well worth the effort.

Cost is another consideration. Local shows, such as church and school bazaars, are usually affordable - as low as 10.00 per booth. Well-attended, popular venues can be upwards of 200.00 or more. Many popular antiques and collectibles shows last several days, making it necessary to find overnight accommodations. Many flea markets are ongoing during the warm weather, so you'll have to be prepared to set up and tear down many times during this period.

Start looking for popular shows well before December to take advantage of holiday sales. These events fill up fast. Requesting a registration form and sending the necessary fees and info ensures you'll snag the most coveted booth placements.

For listings of craft fairs, flea markets and antiques/collectibles shows in your area visit the following websites:

- www.craftlister.com
- www.festivalnet.com
- www.craftyshowsandfairs.com
- nationalcraftshows.com

Craft Malls

This option is becoming more popular among crafters. Empty buildings are being turned into indoor flea markets, and antiques, collectibles and craft malls. Crafters rent booths from mall owners and set up permanent shop. The mall owner charges a monthly booth rental fee - the cost depends upon the size of the booth. Some mall owners charge an additional percentage of sales on top of the rental fee. It usually isn't necessary to be present during business hours, as mall owners themselves or assistants man a central register and keep track of sales. Asking mall owners if they'd consider reducing the rental fee in exchange for operating the register is always a cost-saving option.

Craft Parties

The craft party is becoming more popular with artists wishing to sell their handiwork. Begin by organizing a party in your home. Be sure to have plenty of actual products available for partygoers to view. Create and print brochures and/or price lists on your computer so participants can easily refer to prices, colors, sizes, and other options. Make your craft parties memorable and fun by serving refreshments and playing party games.

As your craft items and parties become more popular, consider branching out to include incentives for friends and family to host their own parties. Percentage discounts, free merchandise and gift certificates encourage people to sell your items via parties.

Whether you choose to sell your artwork or other crafts via online seller, your own website, craft mall, flea market or parties, there are certain things to take into consideration:

- Update items frequently. People will check back often if they know your inventory increases frequently.
- Keep careful records of best-sellers and flops, as this will allow you to concentrate on more popular items.
- Be prepared to haggle with buyers when in a flea market setting. People almost always expect this. Set prices slightly higher to allow for this.
- Stage craft booths attractively and creatively. Use props to make your booth more inviting to visitors.
- Don't set it, then forget it. Visit your craft mall booth often to update, refresh and enhance the look.

Domestic

Most modern households are dual income. This means couples, especially those with small children, have little time to cook, clean, perform ordinary pet care, garden, wash vehicles, and take care of other household chores. Additionally, many of us are now part of the "sandwich generation", where couples are not only taking care of children, they're tending to the needs of aging parents at the same time. Talk about stressful!

This opens up a huge market for *domestic* help. When most people think of the word "domestic" they think of maids, butlers and nannies. While a certain portion of the population are fortunate enough to employ full-time maids and nannies, most are not. Much of the time, picking up some of the household slack for overworked parents is all that's needed. It becomes easy to find your entrepreneurial niche when you think outside the box.

You may wish to limit yourself to catering to one specific segment of the population - for example, working only with senior citizens. There's certainly no shortage of clientele in this category. Or, you might think of labeling yourself as the go-to person for the last minute care of family members, pets, and/or residences.

Keeping your options open ensures you'll have a steady supply of customers. No two families are alike. Everyone has different priorities and needs. Designing a custom plan, based upon the individual requirements of each client will ensure you'll remain in business for many years to come. Clients will come to appreciate your ability to remain flexible, which often results in the purchase of additional services.

Be sure to let your clients know the full scope of your services. Often, you may be able to provide services they may not have even thought of utilizing. Offer affordable packages, which combine several options, perhaps at a discount. Thinking on your feet is the key to success! Consider the following domestic-related business ideas as jumping off points.

Daycare Provider

I'm not talking about your typical children's daycare. Although that can be an admirable and much needed business to embark upon, it certainly does not come without a host of red tape, regulations, rules and an assortment of other issues. I'm talking about a business where you, the daycare provider, go to the client to take care of children and the elderly.

Who are your clients?

- Stay at home moms who need a break, or a chance to get chores and errands done.
- Parents of special needs children who need an extra set of hands.
- Parents wishing to accomplish some holiday shopping out of the view of prying eyes.
- Parents on vacation with children, in need of some much needed adult time.
- Adult children of elderly, ailing parents who simply need time to recharge.
- Pet parents who need someone to make sure Fido gets his exercise.

You can find potential clients in a number of ways. Word of mouth is a tried and true method of gaining a steady clientele. Show up on time, go above and beyond the call of duty, and keep children (or elderly adults) safe, entertained and happy and you'll have no shortage of repeat customers.

Other ways to find clients include:

- Putting up flyers
- Contacting local churches to let them know you're available to assist parishioners
- Advertising in local newspapers and on online classifieds

Providing on-call daycare services is especially helpful to overburdened families. Last minute appointments, sick children and mandatory overtime have a way of happening at the most inopportune times. You can step in to provide peace of mind and comfort to stressed-out families.

Make a list of the services you'll provide. This will help you as well as your clients. You may decide to include running errands, driving clients to appointments, medication reminders, cooking and light cleaning. Having a comprehensive list will avoid any misunderstandings later.

Create a bag of goodies to take along to clients' homes. A tote bag containing crayons, coloring books, games, puzzles and picture books will entertain children and keep them from becoming bored. If you choose to care for the elderly, pack your bag with books, a deck of cards, games and puzzles.

What you charge for this service will depend greatly on your specific geographical location. Large cities tend to command higher rates. Check around to see what similar services are charging. Or, you can decide how much you'd like to earn per hour and go from there. Obviously, the more services you include, the more you should charge.

House Sitter

Everyone needs a break from the daily grind to recharge and revitalize. Most families try to make a point of taking at least one vacation trip a year. Yet, it can be difficult to truly relax if you're worried about break-ins, broken pipes, power outages and any number of disasters. Leaving a responsible, reliable house sitter in charge can greatly reduce stress for homeowners.

Not all house sitters spend the night in the home, but most do. You'll find that homeowners prefer this arrangement. After all, just as things can go wrong during the day, household mishaps can also occur at night.

As long as you're house sitting, you may wish to offer other services such as lawn mowing, pool cleaning, plant watering and light housecleaning, and charge accordingly. Just be sure that all parties are clear about what services are included to avoid misunderstandings later.

It must be mentioned here that we unfortunately live in a society where it is not uncommon for people to sue for any number of reasons. Generally, as a sole proprietor, you do not need to be bonded. Yet, you may run across potential clients who insist that you do so. Try not to be offended or put off by this. Advertising yourself as a bonded house sitter is a good marketing feature. It's also affordable - usually around $50 per year, which is a small price to pay to give yourself and your clients peace of mind.

Go over a detailed checklist with clients. Be clear about the handling of food consumption, and electricity and cable usage. It's imperative that you finalize all of these details beforehand. You want the house sitting experience to be enjoyable and valuable for both parties.

As with the *Daycare* category above, find potential clients by word of mouth, distributing flyers and posting ads. It's also advantageous to join local and national house sitting associations, as these are valuable resources. Search the internet for associations in your area for more information.

As you acquire more customers, keep careful track of scheduled house sitting gigs to avoid conflicting or overlapping bookings. Purchase a date book to maintain a proper schedule.

When deciding how much to charge for house sitting services, be aware that $30 - $50 per day is average. Of course, if more services are added you should raise the rate accordingly.

Pet Sitter

Many business people find it necessary to work long hours and to attend frequent business trips. Many business people are also pet owners who are often forced to board their dogs and cats in expensive kennels. Having the more personal alternative of a caring, attentive pet sitter take care of Fido in their absence can ease the minds of many pet owners.

It usually isn't necessary to stay in the client's home while they're away in order to take care of their pet. Although, you may wish to combine pet sitting services with house sitting services. The number of visits per day will depend upon the pet's individual needs. Often, pet owners prefer at least two visits per day.

As a pet sitter, you will be filling pet bowls, giving bathroom breaks for dogs, cleaning cat pans for cats, walking dogs, and providing mental stimulation such as playing and petting for both cats and dogs.

As with house sitting, you may wish to be bonded, since you will have access to clients homes while they're away. Remember, being bonded is a highly affordable marketing tool.

Find potential pet sitting clients by:

- Having business cards printed and asking local pet shops to allow you to leave a few with them
- Creating eye-catching flyers and posting on local bulletin boards
- Letting local veterinarian clinics know you're available for pet sitting their pet patients
- Posting ads in local newspapers and on online classifieds websites
- Telling friends and family about your pet sitting services

Depending on the duties required, geographical location and the length of the visit, pet sitters can expect to earn anywhere from $10 - $75 per day or $15 - $35 per visit. Consider offering discounts for customers wanting several visits per day. For example, you can charge $35 for two visits, and $45 for four visits.

Obviously, pet sitters should be animal lovers. Be sure you're comfortable around dogs, regardless of size. It's always a good idea to meet with potential clients and their pets in their home environment to get a sense of the pet's behavior. Never accept a pet sitting gig that might put you in danger. Finally, be sure to read pet care books and training manuals to keep yourself updated.

Professional Organizer

Do friends and family often compliment your organizational skills? Is your favorite saying, *"A place for everything and everything in its place"*? Do you always seem to find yourself drawn to the totes, bins, baskets and shelving isles at your local supercenter? Have friends and family ever said, *"If only I had the time to organize. I bet you could get this place in ship shape in no time!"* If you said yes to any of these questions, and you thrive on turning chaos into order, you'd probably make an excellent professional organizer.

US News and World Report recently named professional organizing as one of the top 20 home based businesses. And there's good reason for this. As with most other household chores, busy, two income families have little time to efficiently organize their homes. However, for any household to run smoothly it's imperative to have things in proper order. That's where you come in.

As a professional organizer you can help clients:

- Reduce clutter
- Develop comprehensive filing systems
- Make better use of available space
- Design the most effective storage plan for them
- Make better use of their free time

You can choose to specialize in residential organizing, office organizing, or both.

As a professional home organizer you can choose to limit your services to organizing:

- Closets
- Basements
- Home offices
- Craft rooms
- Children's rooms
- Nurseries

As a professional office organizer you can specialize in:

- Getting rid of clutter
- Digital or hard copy filing systems
- Optimal space planning
- Financial records management

You'll find that different clients have different needs, situations and preferences. Offering free initial consultations is the key to developing custom organization plans for your customers. Schedule a generous amount of time to do a complete walk-thru to determine the best way to proceed. Ask customers what their specific organizational goals are and go from there. Potential clients will be assured that you provide the one-on-one attention they desire. Lastly, you may wish to offer your clients low-cost, or no-cost follow-up visits to be sure they're staying organized.

As with most other service-related businesses, earnings will depend on geographical location. Professional organizers in large cities charge more than those in rural areas. Rates run from $40 - $65 per hour or more. Find clients through word of mouth, newspaper and online ads, and by posting flyers.

Virtual Assistant

Many more Americans than ever are working from home. After all, isn't that why you're reading this book? You want to be among the millions of people who've left the daily grind behind and are making a living via a home office. Right? Virtual assistants are more in demand now than ever before. They provide a cost-effective solution to entrepreneurs who struggle to manage daily business operations by themselves, yet who don't have enough work to justify hiring a full-time (or even part-time) employee. Additionally, virtual assistants are considered independent contractors, therefore business owners don't have to concern themselves with withholding taxes, providing insurance or other employer responsibilities.

Virtual assistants usually provide services such as appointment scheduling, billing, data entry, direct mailing, advertising management, and any number of other tasks. Much will depend on the individual needs of the client.

The great thing about being a virtual assistant is clients don't have to be local. Skype, FaceTime, Google Hangouts and other video-based services make it possible for virtual assistants to meet with clients hundreds, or even thousands, of miles away.

Earnings will vary according to the services provided, hours worked, etc. Most virtual assistants charge by the hour, although charging by the project is also an option. Rates vary anywhere between $20 - $100 per hour, so the potential to make a good living as a virtual assistant certainly exists.

Apartment Cleaner

Rather than discussing *house* cleaning, we've chosen to zero in on *apartment* cleaning. That's because there are more benefits to gearing your cleaning services towards apartments, rather than towards full-scale houses. Those benefits include:

- Apartments are typically smaller than houses and can be completed in less time
- They are grouped together, greatly reducing travel time
- It's possible to make on-going cleaning arrangements with complex owners
- You can potentially clean several apartments per day, which greatly increases your earnings

Finding clients is a breeze if you live in a heavily populated city. Make the rounds of nearby apartment complexes. Visit apartment rental offices to let them know about your business and ask if you can hang flyers on their bulletin boards.

Often, clients will ask that you bring your own cleaning supplies, so figure this into your start-up costs. Discuss the option of using client-owned equipment (bulky items like mops, buckets, vacuums, etc.) with clients to limit or eliminate the need to lug heavy cleaning equipment up stairs. Many clients will be agreeable.

Be sure to make an initial visit prior to giving a quote. Not all clients and apartments are created equal. You'll soon find that some apartments will need minimal cleaning, while others will need extensive scrubbing. You'll probably wish to break down your services into light and heavy cleaning. Generally, those are:

Light cleaning:
- Dusting
- Vacuuming carpets
- Bathroom cleaning (tub, sink and toilet)
- Mopping floors
- Cleaning kitchen countertops
- Wiping down stovetops

Heavy cleaning:
- Oven cleaning/stovetop scrubbing
- Window washing
- Ceiling fan washing
- Refrigerator cleaning

It's a good idea to create a contract, so that both parties understand what services are included, how often and when you will perform services, and price. Consider becoming bonded. Just as with house and pet sitting, you will be alone in clients' homes and bonding protects both parties.

Personal Chef

Do friends and family consistently compliment you on your culinary skills? Are you a master at preparing healthy, delicious meals your entire family loves? Is spending time in the kitchen, chopping, dicing and slicing your idea of a good time? Then a personal chef business is ideal for you!

Notice I'm not suggesting you start a *catering* business. Catering comes with a host of strict regulations imposed by local board of health departments. Bringing your residence up to code can be expensive. You want to make money, not spend it. Being a personal chef is different than catering in that you prepare the food at the client's residence, thus eliminating the need to adhere to any health code regulations. You should, however, consider taking a food handling safety course. Doing so protects you and your clients, and is also a great marketing feature.

Many families are strapped for time and this unfortunately leads them to unhealthy eating habits. There's a reason fast food is so popular - it's convenient and it's cheap. Yet, if given the choice of serving their families delicious, nutritious meals, most moms would jump at the opportunity. Who wouldn't want to come home to a home-cooked meal after a long day at work?

Don't think you have to slave away in a stranger's kitchen every night of the week to be a personal chef. Meal prep is the key to running this business efficiently and effectively. You only need to spend a few hours at the client's home, preparing and cooking a week's worth of meals, store them in airtight containers and put them away in the family fridge (or freezer). Busy moms can take meals out as needed, heat them up in the microwave and enjoy them at the family dinner table!

It's essential to work directly with each family to establish their individual tastes, diet restrictions and health limitations. A targeted checklist works well and ensures that you consistently keep in mind these requirements when planning meals. Preparing meals the entire family can and will eat will be your biggest challenge. Gluten, salt, sugar, and other restricted ingredients must be taken into account.

Begin by taking stock of your current pantry items. Chances are, you already have many of the necessary items in your own kitchen. Most families own pots, pans, knives, blenders, etc. and will be more than happy to have you use them. This greatly reduces your start-up costs. You may wish to supply the airtight containers yourself, and add these to your service fees. Or, families may wish to purchase their own containers. Either way, you should figure these things into what you charge for your personal chef services.

Since this is a fairly new type of business, income can vary. Check around locally to find out what others are charging for this service. Or, you can determine cost by deciding how much you'd like to earn per hour and charge accordingly. You may wish to supplement your income by offering party planning and hosting, and cooking classes.

Mobile Auto Detailer

There's no denying that most people love their cars. We spend thousands of dollars on our vehicles and want them looking good long after we leave the dealership. If you enjoy making your own car look shiny and new you may wish to consider auto detailing.

While many onsite auto washing and detailing businesses exist, not many mobile versions do. Taking your auto detailing business on the road benefits everyone. As the business owner, you'll benefit by eliminating costly overhead in the form of property rental and all the utility expenses that come along with it. Customers will greatly benefit by eliminating the need to take time out of their busy schedules to transport their vehicles to a detailing facility.

Your biggest expense will be your cleaning supplies. Search online for wholesalers, as this will save you hundreds of dollars in the long run. Aside from car cleaning supplies, you'll need totes and other carriers to conveniently store your tools of the trade in your trunk or truck bed.

Costs for an exterior car wash and wax can vary anywhere from $30 - $150, depending upon geographical location. Car detailing, which can take more than 3 hours, can cost anywhere from $300 - $500. If you intend to offer emergency services for clients who find themselves needing last minute car cleaning services, you can charge significantly more.

Find clients by posting flyers, and placing ads in newspapers and online advertisements. Have business cards made and ask local car parts stores for permission to leave a few with them.

Assembler

Talk about a niche business - a very valuable niche business at that! Just about everything we purchase in a store or online comes in a box with a thousand parts and one hard-to-follow instruction sheet. For instance, if you're a wiz at putting IKEA furniture together, then this service is for you. If you scream, swear and cry a little when you see a UPS truck pull up to the curb, then you should probably move on.

Sure, certain supercenters will assemble items for you - when they can fit it into their schedule. But then you still have to figure out how the heck you're going to get it home. And, this isn't an option with an online purchase. There are plenty of people willing to pay someone to put furniture, shelving, and other items together. The elderly, in particular, often find the process difficult (think about offering a senior citizen discount).

Consider offering an express service - *the big game is starting soon and the TV stand absolutely needs to be assembled before the party kind of thing* - for an additional fee of course. Charge according to the complexity, size, number of parts, etc.

Additionally, you can offer an electronics installation service. Many people have no clue how to set up a surround sound system or home theater system. If you're familiar with the process, then you can get paid to do it for clients.

Find customers via word of mouth, flyers, and online and print ads. This is definitely a valuable service with a reasonable earnings potential.

Freelance Writing

Often when people think of freelance writing they think of novel writing. While you can make writing a string of novels your goal, you'll definitely want to branch out into other writing outlets or you'll find yourself having a very rough go of it. Better yet, continue working on your first, second or third novel while you contribute your content elsewhere.

It's not necessary to have a master's degree in English or a degree in journalism. However, you had better have a way with words, and proper grammar and spelling skills - without having to rely on spell check. A talent for dogged research is also necessary, since you won't always be personally familiar with the subjects you'll be writing about.

You may decide to choose a writing niche - press releases, articles, Web copy, etc. On the other hand, you may decide to keep your options open. Learn as much as possible about your area of expertise, since staying current on writing trends is crucial in this business. Join online writer's groups, as these can be of enormous value to you and your writing.

Lastly, do not sell yourself short. Far too many people undervalue writers as a whole. This unfortunate trend will continue as long as there are writers who are happy to be paid a dollar or two for a 500-word article. As in everything else, you get what you pay for, yet there are some clients who think it's acceptable to pay writers pennies for their hard work, even if it means they'll get an article that needs extensive editing. If more writers refuse to accept menial pay for their services maybe this trend will finally change.

The following sections discuss some writing-based small business ideas. If you have a way with words and enjoy living a somewhat secluded lifestyle, freelance writing might be a logical choice.

Article Writer

Online article writing has gotten a bad reputation in recent years. So-called content mills were quite fond of luring potential writers in with promises of either generous rates per article, or unrealistic revenue sharing programs. Unsuspecting freelance writers soon discovered the only one making money from online articles was the content mill. Fortunately, this trend seems to have died a sudden death and many of the notorious mills (who shall remain nameless) have closed shop. Even with the demise of these unscrupulous predators, there is still a market for quality articles. You just have to be creative.

Businesses and individuals can certainly benefit from strategically targeted articles. Educating the public about a business, musician, photographer, author, etc. via an informative and engaging article can result in dozens of potential leads. Properly key-worded articles, posted on websites and blogs are an excellent method of opening the doors to communication with clients in a way that might not be possible via other venues. Most business owners and individuals understand this. If they don't, it can be part of your marketing strategy to inform them.

To find clients, post online ads advertising yourself as an article writer. Most potential clients will ask to see samples prior to hiring you. Write a few free articles for friends and family to build your portfolio, then include links to these articles in your resume, and on your website or blog. DO NOT fall for the "send us some samples of your work" or "write a sample article for us" nonsense. These are usually scammers looking to score free content from unsuspecting newbies. Don't get taken by these thieves.

Charge by the word or by the article. Rates vary and can be as low as 2¢ per word or $2 per 500-word article. These, of course, are extremely low rates and you'll have a difficult time making money if you stick with them. Every time a freelance writer agrees to accept such low wages for their writing they drag the rest of the writing community down with them. It can take hours to properly research, write, edit, proofread and upload an article. Would you accept 50¢ an hour to work anywhere? Of course not! Don't accept it for your writing. You'll attract higher quality clients if you stay firm and demand reasonable rates for your work.

Press Release Writer

Some people have the misconception that the press release is dead. This is absolutely false. While press release submission techniques may have changed over the years, press releases themselves are still alive and well. They remain necessary advertising tools for savvy business owners and individuals.

It's true that you can still mail (or personally deliver) a press release to local radio stations, television studios and newspapers. You can certainly do this, since most local media outlets continue to share press release content. However, it's much more efficient and effective to electronically submit a press release to hundreds (if not thousands) of press release submission sites. Some sites are free, some are affordably priced and some are expensive. Regardless, press release submission websites are BIG business because content providers enjoy having access to thousands of newsworthy press releases to share on their websites. These submission sites are a treasure trove of information Having said all of this, you may wish to concern yourself with press release *writing* only and not offer press release *submission* services. Formatting and adding links can sometimes be a nightmare. It's also a time-consuming process. Although, you could certainly offer press release submission services for an additional fee.

The key thing to remember when writing a press release is to find a newsworthy hook to create a sense of timeliness and urgency. You need a valid reason for writing a press release, otherwise you're just writing an article. Things like a new business venture, grand opening, grand reopening, tour announcement, book release or website launch are great press release topics.

There is a definite formula and template to use when writing a press release. I won't go into the particulars here. There are many books, articles and websites strictly devoted to press release writing. Once you get the hang of it, you'll have no trouble firing off several professional-looking press releases each day.

A well-written press release can command big bucks from clients. We've seen people charge anywhere from $20 (on the extremely low side) to $1,500 and more. $300 - $500 seems to be the average. As you gain more experience and grow your press release portfolio you'll find you can charge more. As with article writing, consider writing a few free press releases for friends and family. This will give you the necessary experience and press release content to add to your portfolio.

Web Content Writer

Have you ever visited a website and wondered, *"Who the heck wrote this stuff, a five-year-old?"* Immediately, in your head, you reconstruct the Web content to make it more user-friendly. If so, you just might have a knack for Web content writing.

Web content writing is truly an art form. Internet surfers have little time for fluff pieces or long-winded ramblings. They visit sites to find information and if they don't find what they're looking for in the first few seconds they're off to visit the next website. Website owners know this. Unfortunately, website owners are not always skilled at content writing. They might know what their business or personal message is, but they can find themselves struggling for the perfect words to quickly convey that message to their visitors.

Knowing exactly what your client is looking to accomplish with their website is crucial to becoming a success in this writing niche. Once you produce quality content for a client, you'll find them relying on you more and more, which results in a steady income for you.

You can charge by the hour, by the word, or by the page. Rates vary widely and are quite comparable to those of article writing. If you decide to create a website for your web content writing business you darn well better be sure it's perfect. Potential clients will judge your abilities by what they read on your website.

Resume Writer

There is no better time than now for freelance writers to become proficient at resume writing. The current job market has created no shortage of employment candidates looking for a competitive edge over their fellow job applicants. They know how necessary a well-structured, professional-looking, comprehensive resume is to grabbing a potential employer's attention and maintaining it long enough to make a split-second decision. On average, an employer (or HR associate) will spend all of 7 seconds looking at a resume. It's critical for resumes to communicate as much pertinent information in one or two pages.

Rather than think of resume writing as a way to cash in on the high unemployment rate, think of it as a way to assist stressed-out, overwhelmed men and women who are searching for any way possible to put food on the table for themselves and their families. Compassion, understanding and patience will go a long way when dealing with this segment of the population. There is no greater satisfaction than hearing that you've helped someone, albeit in a small way, to secure gainful employment.

Resume writing service fees vary across the country, but you can expect to charge anywhere from $50 - $300 for a two-page resume and upwards of $500 for a resume package that includes cover and thank you letters, job listings and other bells and whistles.

Email Campaign Creator

Writing an email (particularly an email subject line) often takes a certain amount of marketing knowledge. Launching an effective email campaign can be an expensive venture for entrepreneurs. While knowing your target audience is a critical factor in making sure your campaign doesn't fall flat, the content is just as important to a campaign's success. No one wants to waste money on ineffective, poorly phrased wording.

Think for a moment how much spam lands in your email every day. Sometimes our spam settings work and sometimes they don't. We often sign up for online subscriptions and then we forget about them. However, the email marketer hasn't forgotten. He or she is counting on you to open and read their pearls of wisdom, which you won't if it lands in your spam box. Now, imagine yourself as the creator of email marketing content. Think about what you would write to ensure that first, your words don't end up being designated as spam. And second, your intended target actually opens and reads your content instead of simply hitting the delete button.

It's necessary to work closely with the campaign creator to be sure what message he or she is trying to get across. As with almost all other written content, you'll often need to make revisions on the original copy. Be sure to include the number of revisions you'll allow before charging extra (two revisions is usually standard).

You can charge by the word, by the copy or by the hour. Just be sure all parties understand what's expected and included prior to beginning in order to avoid any misunderstandings later.

Newsletter Writer

This skill is similar to email campaign writing, but on a larger scale. Your clients will be business owners and individuals seeking to stay in touch with existing customers, as well as those looking to obtain new customers. A well-written, properly targeted newsletter can take several hours to write and perfect. Today's newsletters usually contain photos, graphics and several clickable links. This is time-consuming work. Additionally, a certain amount of artistic flair is required to create a visually appealing newsletter. Text, photos, column placement and links can make or break a newsletter.

It's important to note that newsletter-writing services do not necessarily include newsletter mailing. Although you may wish to include this as an extra add-on. There are several newsletter marketing and list management services. Some are free, as long as you maintain a "small" list of subscribers (usually under 2,000). Others charge a fee. MailChimp is an excellent place to start.

As with most other writing services, many potential clients will want to see samples of your work before hiring you. Start by writing your own newsletter to get a feel for the process. Then you can offer to create newsletters for friends and family members. Non-profits are always looking for affordable newsletter writers. You can even consider doing freebies for non-profits whose work you admire.

Social Media Manager

Social media is an extremely effective and necessary marketing tool that every entrepreneur and business owner should be utilizing. Sharing really is caring. If you care about your business (and this includes your writing business) then you need to share what you're up to.

Many business owners create Twitter accounts and Facebook pages and then realize they don't know what to do with them. Attracting new followers and likes, and keeping people interested and engaged takes time and skill. Business owners want to spend their time conducting business, not figuring out how to be clever in 140 characters or less. You can assist them with this task.

No one expects you to sit at your computer 24/7, tweeting and posting. Register for a *HootSuite* account and manage social media sites from there. HootSuite offers both free and paid accounts, so you can give it a try at no cost.

The key to effective social media engagement is maintaining that fine line between self-promotion and everything else. It's essential to include informative, entertaining and relevant tweets and posts. No one wants to follow or like someone who is always screaming about how wonderful they are and how everyone should buy their product. Self-centered, repetitive tweets and posts will get you promptly unfollowed or deleted.

Spend some time looking at successful Twitter accounts and Facebook pages to get an idea of what's working. You'll spot these, of course, by the large amounts of followers and likes. You should begin to see a pattern of tweets and posts.

As a social media manager, not only will you be writing the tweets and posts for your clients, you'll also be posting them. Facebook provides valuable page insights for pages with over 30 likes. Pay careful attention to these, since they'll indicate what's working and what's not.

Knowledgeable social media managers are in high demand, therefore they can charge thousands of dollars for their services. However, when starting out, you'll need to keep your fees lower. Charging by the month (to be paid one month in advance) is best. Fees range anywhere from $50 - $2,000 per month and depend on the services involved. Simple tweeting and posting will certainly be less expensive than a full-scale consultation and marketing campaign.

Professional Bio Writer

The internet is an essential marketing tool, to be accessed and utilized by businesses, celebrities, entrepreneurs, authors, musicians, etc. How we project ourselves to the public via the internet can mean the difference between success and failure. LinkedIn, Twitter, Facebook, blogs, personal websites and business websites are all online vehicles designed to let consumers, clients and customers know who we are and what we stand for. It's crucial that professional bios present us in the most advantageous light. Unfortunately, many people don't have a clue how to write a well-structured, flattering bio, free of grammar and spelling mistakes.

Your job, as a professional bio writer, will be to gather as much pertinent information as possible about your clients. You can do this via Skype, Google Hangouts, or by emailing clients a detailed questionnaire. It's important that you know where the bio will be used, since many sites limit the number of characters in a bio. You can offer varying lengths:

- Long bios (400 -600 words)
- Medium bios (100 words)
- Short bios (50 words)
- Two sentence bios (140 characters, helpful for Twitter use)

You can offer a package that includes all of the above, or charge per bio. Fees for this service are often per word, or per bio and are usually comparable to article writing fees.

eBook Writer

I'm not talking about novel writing. You can certainly do this, but it takes a great deal of time to complete a book. And, even after you've gone through the process, there's no guarantee you'll make money doing it. Non-fiction eBook writing is the way to go.

Who needs non-fiction eBooks? Business owners are constantly searching for unique and effective ways to get their business message across to consumers. Free PDF eBooks are excellent marketing tools. However, not all entrepreneurs have the expertise or time to write a book. That's where you come in. As a freelance writer, you should consider adding this service to your writing portfolio.

Finding clients isn't difficult - it simply takes some creativity. Begin with local businesses. Make a list of potential industries. From there, break the list down further with individual businesses. Create a sales pitch letter explaining the benefits of offering potential customers eBook freebies.

For example, a foundation repair company can offer customers an eBook explaining how to detect foundation problems, foundation repair options, choosing a foundation repair company, etc. An eBook written for a fitness center can focus on designing the right fitness plan, eating healthy to stay in shape, assessing individual fitness goals, etc. A pet grooming business can give away eBooks that discuss pet health, keeping pets cool in the summer, choosing the right pet food, and other important information for pet owners. Creativity, geared towards your target market, is the key.

From there you can personally visit local businesses or send out emails. Just be sure not to be spammy. Placing ads online or in local newspapers is also an option. Be prepared to offer examples. To do this, consider writing one or two brief eBooks for entrepreneurial friends or family at no cost. Share excerpts with potential clients. These eBooks quickly add to your eBook portfolio. You can also write your own eBook explaining the benefits of eBook freebies to businesses and give these away to potential customers.

What you charge to write business eBooks will depend on your current rate per word, page, etc. It will also depend on how much research is involved. Be sure to take your time into account so that you are compensated accordingly.

My book, *How To Write, Publish and Market Your eBook*, has much more information on eBook writing.

As you can see, there are many ways to capitalize on your proficient wordsmith skills. The important thing to remember is that not all of your clients will have the same needs. It's your job to decide what types of content will be most beneficial for them. Position yourself as the go-to person for business owners looking for interesting, engaging and professional subject matter. If you consistently produce quality work, keep up to date on marketing trends and deliver your work on or ahead of schedule, you'll have no shortage of clients.

Writing-Related

If you're in love with words, possess a set of hawk eyes that can spot a misplaced comma a mile away and don't mind reading for hours at a time, then you have a host of small business opportunities just waiting for you to explore.

Contrary to what some will have you believe, you do not need a degree of any sort to be an editor or proofreader. Plenty of people without degrees make a comfortable living in this line of work. What you do need, however, is an excellent command of the English language, and impeccable grammar, spelling and syntax skills.

Aside from editing and proofreading, we've added a few other writing-related services you may not have thought of, since they are somewhat new to the publishing world.

Editor/Proofreader

Many people think proofreading and editing are identical processes, but they aren't. Proofreading is a *part* of editing, in that it checks a document for spelling, grammar, punctuation and syntax errors. Editing *includes* proofreading, but goes even further. Editing involves checking to be sure the overall document makes sense and has no inconsistencies. Editing often involves several revisions. It may mean that entire portions of the manuscript are altered or even deleted during the process.

Editing is usually the first phase in the process of getting a manuscript ready for publishing. Proofreading is often used to catch any errors that might have been missed during the editing process.

You must have exceptional grammar, spelling and syntax skills to make a living as a professional proofreader or editor. Don't believe the naysayers who insist you need an English degree, or experience working at a major book publishing company. As stated previously, there are many people without degrees who make a comfortable living editing and proofreading. If you feel you're lacking in any of these abilities, all is not lost. There are hundreds of books that can help you build your expertise in these areas.

Editing and proofreading fees vary. Some editors and proofreaders charge by the page. These fees average around $1.00 per page. Some charge by the letter. Per letter fees are anywhere from 2¢ to 20¢. The final cost depends greatly on the amount of editing needed, subject matter, number of revisions included and several other factors. Keep this in mind when quoting prices.

You don't have to just edit and/or proofread book manuscripts. Whitepapers, press releases, Web content, and many other written copy can use a final once over. You can find potential clients via online and print ads, message boards, social media, and through word of mouth.

Beta Reader

Beta reading is a fairly new concept in the world of publishing. A good beta reader can be an invaluable asset to writers. Beta readers read books in draft form and provide authors with feedback. They check for typos, grammatical errors, consistency issues, etc. They often give a detailed, written critique of a book's plot, dialogue, character development and other essential elements. If you enjoy reading and like the idea of being the first to sample new works by up and coming authors then beta reading might be for you.

Contribute to online writing groups and workshops to find clients. Post flyers or business cards at local libraries, colleges and universities to let people know you're available to read and critique manuscripts. Word of mouth via friends and family is an invaluable resource. Beta readers can expect to earn approximately 2¢ - 4¢ per word.

Book Doctor

Book doctors are similar to beta readers. The major difference is that they earn more than beta readers because their services are more extensive. In addition to reading and providing feedback on manuscripts, book doctors provide coaching, critiquing, reviewing, proofreading and editing services. As a book doctor, you may decide to also assist authors with website setup, social media management and event planning for an additional fee. Depending on the amount and type of services you provide, you can eventually command hundreds of dollars per hour. It's best to get some experience under your belt before going this route. Spend time editing, proofreading and beta reading to build up your services portfolio.

Graphic Arts

The introduction of computer programs like Photoshop, Illustrator, InDesign, Corel, Gimp and others has taken art and artwork to a whole new level. The digital age has given artists an entirely new and exciting canvas on which to work.

Many people are under the impression that it's necessary to complete expensive schooling in order to become a graphic designer. At the risk of ruffling a few feathers, I beg to differ. After mastering your chosen graphic design software, you're only limited by your imagination.

You should have a certain amount of artistic abilities, however. Knowing how to design a marketable logo, website banner or header, book cover, etc. that utilizes the most appealing colors, fonts, and graphics comes naturally to some people, but most people can master these skills with practice. If you're one of those people who are genuinely artistic, a business in the graphic arts industry might be for you. The following sections discuss several businesses that capitalize on your creative talents while taking them into the digital age.

eBook Cover Creator

If you have artistic flair or are handy with a camera, you may find your niche here. Many Indie authors actively search for graphic artists who are adept at creating eye-catching, accurate representations of their books.

Familiarize yourself with book cover dimensions, as required by the various online booksellers. For example, according to Amazon, Kindle book covers should be "*a minimum of 625 pixels on the shortest side and 1000 pixels on the longest side...for best quality, your image should be 1563 pixels on the shortest side and 2500 pixels on the longest side.*" You can use these measurements to create sample covers using *Photoshop*, *GIMP* or even *PowerPoint* to show potential clients.

Photographs make wonderful book covers. Use them as backgrounds for book titles and author names, designed with attractive typography.

Print book covers are an entirely different ballgame, as the layout for these are very different from eBook covers. However, you may wish to learn how to create print covers as well since there is definitely a market for them.

eBook covers can be found online from as low as $10, to as high as $500. Create a name for yourself in this rapidly growing niche by providing quality covers at reasonable prices and you should have a steady stream of repeat customers.

Header/Banner Creator

Websites, blogs, online sellers (such as Etsy), LinkedIn and Twitter all offer the opportunity to upload an attractive header. Few business and website owners are skilled enough at graphic arts to create a visually appealing header that allows visitors to know what the site represents at a glance. Choosing and arranging the appropriate colors, graphics and typography is truly an art form.

Working directly with clients to discuss what they wish their custom header to communicate to visitors will eliminate the need for several revisions. Things like color, type style, photos, drawings, etc. are often a matter of personal opinion and are open to personal interpretation. As is the case in any business transaction, narrowing down the particulars will avoid pitfalls and misunderstandings later. Decide how many revisions are included with your price and don't deviate from your decision. This is important since you might eventually encounter a customer who will change his or her mind several times and expect you to provide unlimited revisions.

Header design service fees vary greatly - anywhere from $35 - $100s. Practicing and creating sample headers will give you the experience you need, while building a portfolio of samples.

Banners are similar to headers, but they're often created for promotional purposes. For example, authors who are sponsoring a book release will often have a custom banner created. These are then used on their own websites and sent to bloggers who may be hosting the book release. Other reasons for custom banners might be:

- Introducing a new product or service
- Advertising a current sale
- Promoting an online shop (as with Etsy shops)
- Combining a company message with contact information

Fees for banner creation are generally comparable to those of header creation.

Logo Creator

A custom designed logo sets one company apart from the rest. A well-developed, attractive logo should be memorable and say something about the business it represents. Producing an eye-catching logo takes a certain amount of artistic ability and graphic design know-how. You can offer these services to businesses, entrepreneurs, musicians, artists, etc.

Becoming proficient at using Photoshop and other similar computer software is the first step to mastering the art of logo design. Make several logos to use as samples. Design a few freebie logos for friends and family. Potential clients will want to see your portfolio and this will provide the proper material to do this.

You can find logo design services advertised online for as low as $40. However, it's strongly advised that you don't start your prices any lower than $150 per logo (to include one revision), as most consumers are suspicious (and rightly so) of logo services offered any lower than that. As with most things, consumers know they'll get what they pay for and you definitely want to provide the very best service possible.

Brochure Designer

Businesses and individuals need brochures for promotional events, direct mailings and responses to business inquiries. Savvy business owners understand that maintaining a supply of specifically targeted brochures can significantly boost sales and profits. A brochure designed for a direct mailing would be quite different from a brochure created for a one-time event. It's essential that designers fully understand the purpose of a particular brochure. Determine who the target audience is, as this is an important consideration and will determine color, layout, size, etc. Understanding these elements prior to taking on a job is the key to making the process go as smoothly as possible.

Brochure designers generally do not write ad copy. They concern themselves with design layout only. Nor do they usually edit any provided copy. Although, you can always offer these services for an additional fee.

As a brochure designer you'll need to know about graphic design and typography. While you could purchase expensive desktop publishing software, you're probably not in the position to spend hundreds of dollars for these pricey programs. If you have Microsoft Word, then you're ready to begin designing professional-looking brochures now. Play around with design, fonts, graphics, layout, etc. to get a feel for the process. Create a few samples to show to potential clients. As you progress in your design skills and have fulfilled a few orders, you might consider upgrading to a more advanced desktop publishing program.

Brochure designer fees vary with expertise. Some designers charge by the hour, while some charge by the job. The cost for brochure design depends on size, layout, complexity, etc. In general, prices can be anywhere from $20 to $300 (or higher) per hour, or $30 - $500 per job.

Real Estate

While you *can* take classes to become a licensed real estate broker, that's not what I'll discuss in this section. There are several real estate based niche businesses that can be started with little to no money and require absolutely no licensing or certification.

The average American moves eleven times within their lifetime. That's a lot of packing, unpacking, moving, organizing, home-selling, home-buying, etc. For each of these tasks there exists many opportunities to make money.

Apartment dwelling can be expensive. First month's rent, last month's rent and a one-month security deposit is almost always required. That easily adds up to thousands of dollars. It's imperative that a tenant leave an apartment in the same (or better) condition than it was when they moved in. Unfortunately, some apartment owners deduct a portion of a security deposit for some very minor infractions. It's well worth the effort of completely scrubbing down an apartment prior to moving.

Selling a home takes a great deal of time, patience and creativity. While houses in certain areas of the country are scooped up almost immediately after being placed on the market, others in less popular cities often sit for several months without so much as a nibble. Utilizing every sales tip, trick and technique possible can facilitate the sale of a less than perfect home. A business that assists anxious families in selling a house as quickly as possible is sure to be a welcome relief.

If you've thought about a career in real estate, but weren't willing to devote the necessary time and investment into becoming a real estate agent, the following business ideas should give you some valuable alternative ideas.

Move In/Move Out

This service is in particular demand among apartment dwellers and apartment complex owners. To ensure a timely security deposit refund it's essential that apartment dwellers leave empty apartments in spotless condition. Unfortunately for apartment complex owners, it's not uncommon for some renters to move without notice and leave filthy, poorly maintained apartments behind. Property owners know they can't rent these abandoned apartments until they're cleaned and repaired. Many small apartment complex owners don't have full-time maintenance staff available. You can offer your move in/move out services to both apartment dwellers and complex owners.

The current economy has forced many homeowners to default on mortgages at an alarming rate. Foreclosed homes are often difficult to sell even under the most ideal conditions. However, many bank-foreclosed houses are in various states of disrepair. It's in a bank's best interest to ensure that a house is as clean and presentable as possible. Getting in touch with local banks and realtors to let them know about your move in/move out service is sure to build your client base.

Count on supplying your own cleaning supplies and equipment. You'll also be doing some pretty dirty work. Online wholesale cleaning supply companies are plentiful and can save you money. Keeping a wide array of cleaning products on hand ensures you're ready for just about any job.

Some people will attempt to get a price quote over the phone. Don't ever do this. Always visit an apartment or home prior to giving an estimate. This is the only way to be sure you won't lose money cleaning a residence that takes far longer than expected. You can charge by the hour or by the job. Just be sure to accurately estimate how long a job will take to be sure you make a profit.

Staging Expert

When house hunting, most potential buyers want to walk into a home and envision themselves living in their new environment. Unfortunately, many home sellers aren't aware that family photos, memorabilia and vacation knick-knacks make it impossible for potential buyers to do this. A clean slate is critical to selling a home - yet not so clean that the home looks abandoned. In other words, getting it right takes some design work and know-how.

If you're good at interior design, becoming a staging expert might be an excellent business choice. And, the best thing is you don't need a degree to do it. Knowing how to create a lived-in look without all the personal clutter is the key to this business.

Often, you'll be able to utilize the homeowner's furniture and accessories. However, it's a good idea to accumulate a variety of items to use. Browse antique shops, estate sales, flea markets and yard sales to find unique, attractive pieces.

Be prepared to move some heavy furniture. If you're unable to do this yourself, it helps to partner with someone who can. As an alternative, you can always specify in the contract that all heavy moving is to be done by the homeowner or realtor. It's best that sellers eliminate as much clutter as possible prior to placing a home on the market, so they'll need to do this anyway.

Find potential clients by cold calling realtors and bank loan executives (they handle foreclosures), distributing flyers and handing out business cards. You can charge by the hour or by the job.

Real Estate Photographer

If you own a good camera, love taking photos and know how to use basic photo-editing software, you should consider starting a real estate photography business. Who are your clients? Real estate agents, homeowners, new home developers and others.

Have you ever shopped for a home and gone to a realtor's website only to find blurry, awful photos that leave you cold? People rely on the internet for practically everything nowadays. Narrowing down a home search by sifting through online listings saves consumers stress, travel time and money. Bad photos will not motivate potential homebuyers to visit a home in person. Real estate agents might know how to sell houses, but they might not be great at taking photos. Whether working with a realtor, or searching on their own via the internet, consumers want to see clear, well-lit and accurate photos. That's why your services will be an invaluable asset to your clients.

Always take more photos than you think you could possibly need. This will give you a greater selection to choose from before and after editing. Natural lighting is always best, so try to schedule your shoots during the day.

Consider partnering with a staging expert (see the previous *Staging Expert* section) or adding this service to your business. The idea is to shoot the most flattering photos, but this is impossible if a home is cluttered and messy. We've all seen messy, cluttered homes for sale and wonder what the seller could possibly be thinking.

Find clients by contacting realtors and new home developers (they're looking to sell homes too), distributing flyers and handing out business cards. Be prepared to show samples. A photography website (even a free one like WordPress.com or Blogger) is essential. Remember, people want to see how your photos come across via the internet. Charge for your photography services by the hour or by the job.

Photography Services

Speaking of photography, aside from taking real estate photos (see the previous section) you can offer your services to a variety of clients. Most people don't care if you have a photography degree, they just want the best photos possible of themselves and their loved ones. If you're good with a camera and photo editing software, you're good to go. Cameras have come a long way in terms of cost and capabilities. Digital SLRs take fantastic photos. They can be purchased for a few hundred dollars - even less if you choose a refurbished camera. You might already have one. There are many free and low-cost photo editing software programs available. If you don't already own the software, free online trial versions are almost always available. Download a few and see which one you like best before making a purchase. Or, go with a free software program, such as Gimp. It's free and just as powerful as PhotoShop.

Creating an attractive photography website is a must for this business. Potential clients will want to see your online portfolio before contracting you to take photos. You can save money by using a free website builder. There are many to choose from and this is a perfectly acceptable option for cost-conscious entrepreneurs.

Aside from the typical photography gig, think outside the box when seeking clients. The internet has opened up a huge market for online sellers, marketers and others. I've included the ordinary, as well as the not-so-ordinary photography client in the following sections.

Wedding Photographer

This is probably the number one reason why consumers contract photographers. This is also the most difficult job to pull off. Tension and expectations are on high alert. Everything needs to be perfect. The bridal couple, their parents and the bridal party are all expecting complete perfection and you had better deliver it or you'll find yourself in front of Judge Judy (we've all seen these cases). If you fall apart under pressure, you probably want to steer clear of photographing weddings. While it can be fun to share the day with the happy couple (free food and lots of fun) it can also be stressful.

Word of mouth will probably be your number one method of finding clients. A photo-packed website and business cards are a must. Consider joining an online photography organization to lend credibility to your photography business. Some are free, some are affordable and some are expensive. Many offer certification training. Again, this is certainly not necessary to operate a photography business. However, taking classes at your local community college never hurts. This also keeps you up to date on photography trends.

Baby and Child Photographer

Most of us ooh and ahh over the sight of a precious sleeping infant. Parents want to preserve that infant stage forever and doing it with a gorgeous photo is an excellent way to accomplish that.

The great thing about baby photography is that most of the time your subject will be asleep. The best photos are taken right after birth and up to two weeks. Babies are tiny and are asleep much more than they are awake. Be sure to keep a box of props on hand. Blankets, cute hats, diaper covers (little over pants), baskets, buckets, and other items bring your photos to the next level. Do an online *Etsy* or *Pinterest* search for baby photography props to get ideas.

Since natural light is the most flattering, even for naturally adorable babies, schedule your shoots during the day and take photos near windows whenever possible. You'll want to ask parents to crank up the heat, since a warm room means a toasty, comfy baby who will sleep through practically anything. A space heater works well too.

As a way to build your business portfolio, consider offering free or reduced photo packages to friends and family. Few people can resist the opportunity to have pictures taken of their little one. Find clients via online and print ads, word of mouth or contact new parents via local newspaper announcements.

Pregnancy Photographer

This is becoming a very popular photography niche. There was a time when pregnancy was something women hid behind big, gaudy blouses and dresses. Not anymore. Celebrity magazines are filled with pages of proud, pregnant moms-to-be. This has created a huge market for photographers.

Most modern moms-to-be don't mind showing off pregnant bellies. If you wish to cater to this segment of the population, you'll need to be comfortable with naked or near-naked bodies. The focus of these photos is the pregnant tummy and the best way to show it off is in all its naked glory. Most often, the only covering your subject will have is a filmy, gauzy scarf or piece of fabric. Not only will you need to be comfortable with this, it will also be your job to put your subject at ease.

Online Seller Photographer

Obviously this service will work with local clients only, since the idea is for you to take clear, attractive photos of items other people wish to sell online. Many people sell their own products on eBay, Etsy and other online selling sites. However, they might not be good at taking photos - a definite liability for any online seller. Clear, attractive, accurate photos are essential to online selling.

You might wish to dedicate one room as your photography studio. A room with plenty of natural light is ideal. Clients can then bring their products for you to photograph. As a way to make more money, you may even opt to list the items for the customer - for an additional fee of course.

If you prefer, you could also travel to the client's home. The choice is yours. Affordable photography studio kits are available online. Practically everything you need is contained in one box.

Insurance Photographer

Aside from the real estate photography I discussed in the previous chapter, there exists a wide open market for consumers - taking photos and video for real estate insurance records.

Most homeowners insure their property and its contents. Many apartment dwellers insure their belongings. Most of us hope we never have to file a claim, but unfortunately disasters do occur. Properly documenting homes and belongings can literally save homeowners thousands of dollars in the event that an insurance claim is filed. Insurance companies frequently deny claims based on insufficient documentation.

If you opt to work in this photography niche, your clients will be homeowners, apartment dwellers and insurance companies. You can choose to narrow down your target market and focus on just one of these groups. Regardless of which group you decide to work with, you'll need to be extremely detail-oriented and thorough. You'll need to cross-reference all items included in insurance policies to be sure you have clear photos to match.

If you opt to work directly with insurance companies, you can contact them via phone, email or cold call insurance agents to let them know about your services. If you'd rather work with consumers, you can post flyers, hand out business cards and offer to provide your services free of charge (or at a discount) to friends and family to build your portfolio of clients.

Public Speaking and Instruction

If you possess the gift of gab, you're in luck. A variety of small businesses awaits you. Most people enjoy learning new things. Consumers like to be educated, as well as entertained. If you have a unique skill, a distinctive background or some valuable experience, you should consider entering this niche.

The internet makes it possible to widen your audience as never before. Gone are the days when public speaking engagements required hopping on a plane and criss-crossing the country. Now, all we need to do is turn on our computer to speak directly to hundreds of anxious listeners.

If you think no one will pay to hear anything you have to say you're wrong. Make a list of your skills, experiences, knowledge, expertise, etc. and you'll quickly see how much valuable information you have stored in your noggin. Your life and work experiences provide a wealth of marketable subjects from which to choose. How to distribute this valuable information will be your only concern.

The earnings potential certainly exists here. Popular, in-demand speakers earn thousands of dollars per engagement. The more engagements you have under your business belt, the more money you can command for your services.

The following sections give some suggestions to help you enter the wonderful world of public speaking.

Workshop Instructor

Workshops provide hands-on training to individuals wishing to learn a new skill. For example, if you have mastered the art of origami, and would like to teach others this skill, an origami workshop is an excellent way to share your knowledge. If you're an expert knitter, painter or woodworker, teaching others via workshops is an ideal way to do the things you love while making money.

Don't automatically think you'll need to rent a studio in order to set up your workshops. Remember, you're trying to make money, not spend it. Start slowly by accepting a handful of people per workshop. You can always schedule more than one session per week to increase your income. Doing this keeps things on a smaller scale, and smaller scale means you can work out of a spare room, basement or garage. Plenty of entrepreneurs start out this way. Students are much more concerned with the quality of your instruction, not whether or not you have a state-of-the-art studio.

Draw a few preliminary sketches to get an idea of necessary placement of tables, chairs and other equipment to see which layouts work best for your needs. Don't run out and purchase expensive workbenches and tables. These are easily made with plywood and sawhorses - this is an ideal option when teaching woodworking, jewelry-making, gardening and other similar skills.

You can decide to include all the necessary materials as part of your workshop fee or you can have students purchase these separately themselves. However, if you purchase materials via wholesalers you can sell these to students at a slight markup to further increase your profits.

Find workshop students by word of mouth, posting flyers, handing out business cards, and placing ads in local papers and online.

Training and Seminar Speaker

These are similar to hosting workshops, but can encompass more topics and subject matter and include a certain amount of lecture. Additionally, trainings and seminars have the added benefit of extending to the internet - these are often referred to as *webinars*.

While it's possible to offer workshops online, these are typically better suited for on-site instruction. If you have valuable information and knowledge to share, you should consider offering online or in-person training sessions.

Think you don't possess enough know-how to offer trainings? Think again! Write a list of all your skills, experiences, accomplishments, schooling and other marketable expertise and you'll see just how much information you actually possess. There are many people who would pay good money to learn what you already know.

Trainings and seminars can be one-time events, or several sessions scheduled over a period of weeks. Be sure you have plenty of information to fill several sessions if you decide to go this route. You should prepare a syllabus to keep yourself on track. This also lets students know what is included in your sessions. For your own personal reference, make note of any additional materials you may find helpful: books, articles, online links, slideshows, videos, etc. can all be used as learning materials. If necessary and pertinent, make these available to students by including them in your syllabus.

What types of information can easily be made into training sessions? Here are just a few ideas:

- How to Write Online Articles
- How to Write an eBook
- How to Market Your Business
- How to Be Your Own Social Media Manager
- How to Effectively Use Twitter
- How to Build a Website
- How to Design and Maintain a Facebook Page
- How to Blog for Business

If you're stuck for ideas, try brainstorming by typing a few phrases into your favorite browser. There are bound to be several popular search results suitable for seminars and training sessions.

Beauty, Health and Wellness

I've left this category for last, as I consider some of its subcategories to be more complex and involved than any of the others I've discussed so far. Unlike almost all of the previous ideas, there is a certain amount of investment involved, since you'll definitely want to seek certification training for many of the niches I discuss.

This category is also HUGE. More consumers than ever before are making physical fitness and beauty a priority. The health and diet industry is a multi-billion dollar moneymaker. Many companies claim to be experts in the field of beauty, health and wellness, and say they have consumers' best interests at heart, but many do not. Scammers exist and consumers are beginning to catch on. If you already have a personal passion for getting in shape and eating healthy, while saving money, you have the beginnings of an extremely profitable business.

There are literally hundreds of niche business ideas tucked into this category. While some of these businesses require the operator to be certified, many do not - and most do not require licensing. However, if you want to be taken seriously in your chosen field, which is important to increasing business, you'll want to continually educate and update yourself. Take classes and certifications whenever possible. It will definitely be money well spent.

As already stated, the beauty, health, wellness and fitness field has no shortage of scammers touting false claims of weight loss with minimal effort. The truth of the matter is there is no quick and easy way to get in shape. It takes hard work and determination. Don't be drawn in by phony products that promise to net you thousands of dollars from unsuspecting consumers. Fly by night scams die out quickly. Find a product or service you're passionate about and it will result in a business that will endure for years to come.

I can't stress enough how important it is to thoroughly research your chosen field and to familiarize yourself with your state and local requirements, since these can vary widely. You must be sure you're operating your business under the legal requirements in your area. Insurance is another consideration, as you'll be working with a variety of individuals with a wide array of abilities and limitations. If you do your homework and conduct extensive research you won't experience any interruptions in business operations later.

The following pages discuss just a few suggestions to get you started in this wide-open field.

Trainer/Instructor

Whether you choose to be a personal fitness trainer, or a Zumba, aerobics, Pilates or yoga instructor you'll want to be certified. Even when there is no licensing requirements involved, almost any facility will expect you to be certified. Even when operating independently of gyms, chiropractors' offices and wellness centers, certification lends credibility to your business and instills confidence among consumers. It's difficult to be taken seriously without certification from an accredited source. You can become certified online or in person. Many YMCAs offer certification training, which can be an affordable alternative to pricey schools.

When first starting out, it's common for trainers and instructors to contract with established businesses. You can make arrangements to subcontract through fitness and wellness centers, doctor's offices, alternative medicine clinics, etc. This eliminates your overhead costs, and provides a safe, secure place to see clients. Eventually, or maybe initially, you could make house calls, or set up shop in a refurbished garage, basement or spare bedroom. However, as you might imagine this option is not without a certain amount of risk, so give it careful consideration and take proper precautions before going this route.

Boot camp training has recently become all the rage. Setting up schedules to train clients in local parks is convenient and there's no overhead involved. Most of the time, clients are expected to provide their own equipment - which is usually minimal anyway. Depending on your fitness routine, dumbbells, resistance bands and floor mats are all that's needed. There's a growing trend of military-style boot camp trainers who incorporate a wide variety of discarded items for participants to carry around while they work out - tires, cinderblocks, car parts and other items can become part of a workout routine. Boot camp can be as difficult or as easy as you wish to make it. Consider offering different levels of training to accommodate a greater number of clients. Start a new trend of senior citizen, mommy and me, or pregnancy boot camps.

When it comes to offering wellness training, creativity is critical. You could narrow the scope of your services by targeting one specific consumer group. For example, there's a great deal of medical research proving how important it is for senior citizens to remain physically fit and active. Even a small amount of daily calisthenics makes a world of difference in the mental and physical health of our nation's seniors. On the flip side, it's important for the health of our children that they step away from the television, smart phones and computers. Decide where your passions lie and you'll surely come up with some novel ideas!

Reflexologist

Have you ever noticed that when your feet hurt, your entire body seems to hurt? The same can often be said of our hands. Reflexologists believe there is genuine science to explain this. Reflexology is a holistically therapeutic method of relieving pain by stimulating pressure points on the feet (and hands). Each pressure point is thought to directly correspond to different body parts, organs and glands. In other words, a knowledgeable reflexologist will know exactly which parts of the hands and feet to manipulate in order to relieve pain throughout the body. If you've ever had a good foot rub, then you know how great this feels.

As of this writing, there is no licensing requirement necessary to practice reflexology, with the exceptions of North Dakota, Tennessee and New Hampshire. Thirty-eight states have massage laws, but reflexology is exempt in twenty-six states (meaning no license is required). Finally, in Louisiana and Missouri, reflexology falls under cosmetology licensing laws. Therefore, it is crucial that you research reflexology licensing laws in your state to be sure you are practicing legally.

Aside from licensing, you'll want to find out if your state requires reflexology certification training. Not all states do. However, obtaining certification will add to your credibility, which also increases your marketability.

Reflexology can be a rewarding and lucrative endeavor. Having the ability to relieve the chronic pain your clients may be experiencing is a priceless skill. Many people would gladly pay to rid themselves of headaches, stomach problems and other ailments. There is much statistical information to substantiate the claims that reflexology can accomplish this.

You can make house calls, or contract through fitness centers, nursing homes, wellness centers, day spas and other similar locations. Let local businesses know about your reflexology services. Ask if you can leave flyers and business cards with them. Place ads in local newspapers and on online classifieds sites.

Fashion Coach/Image Consultant

The job market is ever changing. The current unemployment rate is higher than it has been in decades. Competition is brutal. For every job opening there are literally hundreds of candidates desperate to be noticed. Unfortunately, people DO judge a book by its cover. It's critical to look and dress appropriately for job interviews. Candidates might possess the knowledge to secure a well-paying job, but if they show up at an interview looking unprofessional it could very well ruin their chances for a second interview.

If you have a flair for fashion, and friends and family often compliment your sense of style, you may wish to consider a career as a fashion coach or image consultant. Aside from job candidates, you'll be assisting:

- People new to the dating scene
- Local politicians
- Public speakers
- People recently divorced
- Beauty pageant contestants
- Business owners
- Religious leaders
- Brides and bridal parties

You'll be giving style, makeup, accessorizing and other advice to clients. Some ideas might be:

- Closet organization
- Determining appropriate color pallet
- Hair color and hairstyle advice
- Camouflaging body flaws

- Shopping tips

You might wish to consider branching out further to include services such as:

- Improving communication skills
- Developing telephone, email and social media etiquette
- Assertiveness training
- Enhancing public speaking talents

Catering your services to individual clients is best. Each will have their own needs and circumstances. You can charge by the hour or the particular job. Find clients by word of mouth, posting flyers, handing out business cards, and posting online and print ads.

Meal Planner

Today's families are busy with work, school and other activities. Most consumers have little time to properly shop for groceries and prepare nutritious meals. Meals consisting of fatty burgers and fries are the norm for many people. Fast food is often the go-to meal for overwhelmed moms and dads. There's plenty of research to indicate just how bad a fast food diet is, especially for children. High blood pressure, diabetes, obesity and other food-related illness is steadily increasing among Americans. You could be the catalyst who propels your clients to live healthier lives.

Be forewarned, unless you have a degree in nutrition or similar education, be careful not to advertise yourself as such. Your job as a meal planner will be to sit down with the family (or have them fill out a carefully designed questionnaire) to determine what their current eating habits are and what substitutions are necessary and available. For example, it doesn't take a nutritionist to recognize that broiled fish is a far better meal choice than a greasy hamburger. If you've been successful at eliminating fat and cholesterol from your diet, have experienced a significant weight loss and have developed a fitness regimen, you can help others do the same.

It's important that you determine the likes, dislikes and diet restrictions of your clients. Food allergies and sensitivities must be established prior to designing and implementing menu plans. However, it will be part of your responsibilities to encourage even the finickiest of eaters to try new foods.

You may wish to go a step further by preparing healthy meals in clients' homes. Schedule one day a week to do so. You'll need plenty of airtight containers (or use the client's supply) and cooking gear. Shopping services may also be offered. Of course, you'll be charging appropriate fees for these additional services.

Consider becoming certified through The American Culinary Federation or other similar agency. While it is in no way necessary to do so, it does lend a certain amount of credibility to you and your meal planning business.

Plan and prepare a wide variety of nutritious and delicious meals for your clients and you'll have no shortage of customers. Advertise via online and print ads, flyers, business cards and word of mouth.

Fitness Equipment Advisor/Installer

Many people want to get in shape, but they often don't know where or how to begin. Not all workouts are created equal. Some people have certain physical limitations or restrictions, yet they still need a certain amount of exercise as part of a healthy lifestyle. As a fitness equipment advisor you will be assessing your clients' needs, goals, restrictions, etc. For some clients, all that may be needed is a set of dumbbells and pair of resistance bands. Other clients may be more advanced and ready for a multi-faceted workout machine.

Obviously, *you* should be in excellent shape, as you'll be your own best advertisement for a healthy fitness regimen. You should be able to answer any questions clients may have, so be sure to familiarize yourself with current equipment options.

Unfortunately, many store employees aren't as educated on the latest fitness equipment as they should be. Therefore, it may be necessary for you to accompany your clients when they purchase equipment to be sure they are choosing the best equipment for their desired results.

Most people struggle when it comes to installing fitness equipment. As someone who has most likely gone through this process yourself it's an ideal add-on service. Assisting clients with purchasing, transporting and installation of fitness equipment becomes an all-inclusive business that many people will gladly pay for. Additionally, you could offer follow-up services to be sure equipment remains properly maintained after a few months of usage.

Find clients via online and print advertising, handing out business cards, distributing flyers and telling friends and family about your new business venture.

In Summary

These are just a few small business ideas for you to consider. They're meant to pique your interest and encourage you to investigate a business further. Obviously, the information contained in this book regarding business ideas barely scratches the surface of what's involved in any business's daily operations. If any of these ideas strike your fancy, then do your research to see if you have a real desire to pursue it. There are literally thousands of niche businesses waiting for creative entrepreneurs to tap into. All it takes is a great idea, ambition, drive and the will to succeed.

21 Important Questions to Ask Yourself Before Starting Your Business

Now that you have some idea of the type of business you'd like to start, you should ask yourself the following questions before embarking on your new business venture. The answers to these questions will help build the necessary groundwork and avoid some major pitfalls:

1. What is my main motivation for starting a business? (Money? Independence?)
2. Do I know what type of business I want to start?
3. Do I have a well-written business plan?
4. Who is my target audience? (Customers and clients)
5. What products or services will I offer?
6. Do I have a clear idea of my start-up costs?
7. Will I need to apply for a business loan?
8. Who are my competitors?
9. How will my business's services or products differ from those of my competitors?
10. How will my prices compare to my competitors' prices?
11. Where will I operate my business? (Out of my home, rental, etc.)
12. Will I need to hire employees?
13. Where will I get the supplies necessary to run my business?
14. When will I begin to make a profit?
15. How will I support my family and myself before I begin making a profit?
16. What will the legal structure of my business be?
17. What taxes must be paid?
18. Do I need insurance?
19. How will I manage the daily operations of my business?
20. How will I advertise my business?
21. Have I chosen a name for my business?

Consider these questions carefully. If you find that you have any reservations or are having trouble answering several of these questions you may want to rethink your readiness to start your own business. While many small businesses succeed, many fail. Research the answers and begin compiling a business file, detailing your findings. This information will come in handy when you start keeping records. The answers to these questions should be the first page in your file. These questions are addressed in detail in the following sections.

Choose Your Business Structure

There are tax and legal implications involved with the type of business structure you choose. To make it as simple as possible, this book will briefly explore four different types of business structures. You should research your particular state's requirements prior to choosing. Determining a business's structure affects your DBA (Doing Business As) name, which is discussed at length later.

The following information is meant only to give you a general idea of what is involved with the different business structures. Not all businesses are created equal, and your particular circumstance will determine which structure you should choose. The subject of business structure is complex and detailed - far more so than I will go into in this book. You should always consult a legal and/or tax professional prior to proceeding to this extremely important step.

Sole Proprietorship

This is the most straightforward and basic of business structures. It's also the simplest and most commonly chosen structure. All of the businesses mentioned previously are suitable for sole proprietorships, since most are designed to be one-person operations.

As a sole proprietor of a business, you are the only one entitled to any assets. This also makes you solely responsible for any liabilities and debts incurred. You do not need to file any official paperwork as long as you are the only owner. Sole proprietorships status automatically results from your business activities. Many people operate sole proprietorships without even realizing they are doing so - freelance writers, for instance, are sole proprietors. However, you may still be bound by any local licensing and permit requirements. These vary according to your location, so be sure you are operating within these requirements. Research your local requirements for more information. The SBA's licensing and permits tool is invaluable for researching federal, state and local permit and licensing requirements for businesses.

Sole proprietorships are not taxed separately. Your business income is part of your personal income and you report this via the standard 1040 form. You must withhold and pay all income taxes, including self-employment and estimated taxes. Visit the IRS website (www.irs.gov) for more detailed tax information.

There are several benefits to sole proprietorship. These include:

- It's far simpler than other business structures
- It's inexpensive (cost is limited to licensing and permits)
- You have total control over business operations
- There are no separate tax reporting requirements involved

There are some important drawbacks to a sole proprietorship:

- You are personally responsible for any and all liabilities, debts and obligations incurred. This extends to any of your employees

- Financing is generally more difficult. Banks and private investors will often avoid lending money to sole proprietors
- All burden, responsibility, debt and risk is on you

Partnership

Partnerships are structures designed for two or more individuals who operate a single business. Each partner contributes to the business, and each shares all profits and losses. A written agreement is an absolute must for a partnership, since it is essential for the good of the company for everyone to be in accordance so there are no misunderstandings or disagreements later.

There are three types of partnerships:

- General Partnerships
- Limited Partnerships
- Joint Ventures

Each of these partnerships has their specific advantages and disadvantages. If you're considering forming a partnership, it's suggested that you thoroughly research each option prior to choosing. Consult your accountant or attorney for more detailed advice.

Some of the benefits of a partnership are:

- Easy and inexpensive
- Each partner shares an equal investment
- Partners can play off the strengths and skills of each other

Some disadvantages are:

- Personal assets of any partner can be used to satisfy any debts
- The possibility of disagreements and disputes exists
- All profits must be shared equally and this can often lead to discord among partners

Corporation

Corporations are usually reserved for larger companies with several employees. They are more complex and involved to form than sole proprietorships and partners. Additionally, corporations are more costly due to administrative fees, and tax and legal regulations.

Some advantages to forming corporations are:

- Limited liability to shareholders
- It's generally easier to raise funds
- Taxes are filed separately from personal taxes

Some disadvantages are:

- Double taxing sometimes can occur (first when a profit is made, and again when dividends are paid out to shareholders)
- A great deal of paperwork is involved
- Much more costly than sole proprietorships and partnerships

Limited Liability Company (LLC)

This business structure combines the limited liability features of a corporation with the tax efficiency and flexibility of a partnership. Owners of an LLC are considered *members* and these members can be individuals, two or more individuals, corporations or other LLCs. This varies by state, so be sure to verify this with your particular location. LLC members report business profits and losses on their personal federal tax returns.

Some advantages of LLCs are:

- Limited liabilities
- Less expensive than a standard corporation
- Much less paperwork involved than a standard corporation

Some disadvantages are:

- LLC members are considered self-employed and therefore must pay self-employment tax contributions toward Social Security and Medicare
- Many states require that once a member leaves the LLC or passes away, the business must either be dissolved or a new LLC must be formed

You can see that the subject of business structure can be somewhat confusing and complicated. Every business previously discussed would work well as sole proprietorships. However, you should always check with your accountant or attorney before making this important decision.

Naming Your Business

Choosing a name for your business is a critical step not to be taken lightly. Ideally, your business name will eventually become synonymous with who you are and what you do or sell - this is called *branding* and branding is everything in business. Remember, your business name will appear on your logo, website, business cards, flyers and other advertising materials. Make sure it's memorable, catchy and reflects your brand identity. I'll discuss branding in greater detail in the *marketing* section.

Depending on the type of business you choose to start you may decide to use your personal name or you may go with a business name instead. Personal names can be suitable for certain businesses. For instance, many photographers use their own names. However, there is a school of thought that frowns upon using personal names for businesses. To some degree this makes sense, since business names usually appear more professional. As mentioned, business names also help build brand awareness and this is generally more difficult to do with personal names.

A name that reflects your business is an ideal choice. Although it's true that some unusual names have caught on and become popular, as a newbie entrepreneur do you really want to run the risk of confusing potential customers with wacky names that tell them nothing about you, and your company, products and services? Probably not.

Don't forget that we are living in the technology age. Your business name should come across well online. How will it look on the Web and on social media sites? Will you be able to develop an eye-catching logo around your business name? Is it succinct and to the point? Will it appeal to your target market? These are all things to consider.

Once you've decided on a name you must check to be sure that it isn't already in use. A great initial way to do this is to type it into your favorite browser to see what comes up. You should also conduct a trademark search. The U.S. Patent and Trademark Office website contains a search tool located on their site. Don't bypass this step. Trademark infringement can be a costly mistake.

After you've conducted your research to be sure you haven't chosen a business name that's already in use, you'll want to register a domain name as soon as possible to be sure you've secured it. There are people who buy domain names simply because they're popular and then sell them for hundreds of dollars. You want to grab your URL before someone else does. While you're at it you'll also want to register your Twitter and Facebook page accounts. These are all additional steps in building your brand. If you decide to use a name other than your personal name, you'll need to register it.

Registering Your Business Name

This is also known as registering a *Doing Business As* (DBA) name and in most states is required for any businesses operating under *fictitious* or *assumed* names. Check with your county clerk's office to see if this is a requirement in your particular state. However, even if your state does not require a DBA registration, you should definitely file one anyway, since this is an excellent and cost effective way to prevent anyone else from using your business name.

It's important to note that although your business name may contain your personal name - *Susan Barton Professional Writing*, for example - it is still considered a fictitious name and you may need to register it (again, this depends on your state's requirements). From that moment on this will be known as your legal business name and you will need it for any government forms such as licenses, permits and other official documents. You will also need a DBA to open a business bank account.

To register a DBA, contact your county clerk's office to request the proper paperwork. Most states also provide downloadable versions of DBAs in PDF form online, or you can purchase blank DBA forms at your local office supply store. The type of DBA form you need will depend upon your particular business structure, so be sure to select and fill out the correct form.

Fill out the DBA form completely, but do not sign it since you'll need to sign in the presence of a notary. There is a fee for filing a DBA, but it's minimal - usually between $10 and $50, with the average being $25. Be sure to request a certified copy (another $5 or so) to keep in your files.

Writing Your Business Plan

As excited as you might be to jump feet first into the entrepreneurial world, a well-written business plan is a must. Think of a business plan as a blueprint that will help keep you on track at all times. This means your business plan isn't something you write at start-up, stick in a drawer and forget. This means your business plan is something you follow, update and change as needed. Don't try to get away without completing this important step; particularly if you intend to apply for a business loan since all banks will want to see this before even considering lending you money.

Your business plan should be as detailed as possible, yet be to the point. To stay focused and keep your business plan concise, the Small Business Administration (SBA) advises creating the following keyword list:

- Who
- What
- Why
- Where
- When
- How
- How Much

To make the process more simple, and to break things down into bite-size pieces, the SBA suggests labeling seven index cards with the corresponding keywords. Answer each of these keyword questions on each index card. Use these cards as your business plan outline.

There is no specific length when it comes to business plans. The average business plan is usually 30 to 40 pages. Break your business plan down into the following sections:

- Cover Sheet
- Mission Statement
- Business Information
- Marketing
- Financial Documents
- Supporting Documents

This will give you a basic idea of what is to be included in your business plan. Obviously, writing a properly structured, detailed, yet concise business plan is a critical step not to be taken lightly - especially if you will be seeking financial assistance at start-up. It is far more involved and in-depth than I will delve into in this book. The SBA is an excellent resource for entrepreneurs. They have a fantastic online document that explains the business plan writing process in complete detail.

Funding Your Small Business

Now that you know the type of business you want to start, and have written your business plan, you're ready to calculate your start-up costs. Almost all of the small business ideas discussed previously require little to nothing to start. Aside from basic supplies, there are few expenses involved. For the few businesses that do require some start-up capital, you should run to your local bank and apply for a loan, right? Wrong! Depending on how much money you estimate is needed, you do have other borrowing options.

Don't Quit Your Day Job

As excited as you may be to embark upon your entrepreneurial journey, if you're currently working you'll probably want to continue doing so. You may decide you need that financial cushion to continue paying bills as you work to get your new business off the ground. Even if you are not the primary breadwinner, your current job will help fund your initial start-up. Consider setting aside money from each paycheck to use toward business supplies, advertising costs, and other incidental expenses.

Get a Part-Time or Seasonal Job

Working at a part-time job is an excellent way to finance a small business. Many companies actively hire part-timers and often these positions allow for flexible schedules. Working nights and weekends can give you the necessary free time to get your business up and going, while providing you with some extra cash. Hiring tends to increase during holiday season and when the college crowd returns to school. If you time your job search during these periods, you should have no problem finding part-time work.

Dip Into Your Finances

First, you should thoroughly inspect your current finances. Do you have a comfortable nest egg? Do you have a sizeable savings account and/or valuable investments? If you truly believe in your business idea, you should look at it as you would any other investment. While it's not recommended that you leave yourself without a financial cushion, you should consider using some of your own money to fund your business.

You also have the option of:

- Borrowing against life insurance policies
- Borrowing from an IRA
- Using credit cards

These options are not for the faint of heart, and with good reason. There's risk involved with all of them. For that reason, you should resort to them only if absolutely necessary. Regardless of whether you use money from your savings account, or borrow against your assets, you should treat it as you would any other loan. Calculate a repayment plan to pay yourself back in manageable increments and stick with it.

Borrow From Friends and Family

If you don't have a sizeable amount of money in your savings account, or any easily accessible assets, you might wish to consider borrowing from friends and/or family. While no one wants to be the guy who has to approach his father-in-law for money, this is preferable to, and makes more financial sense than, attempting to secure a bank loan.

This is where your business plan comes into play. Although you'll be approaching friends and family, you'll want to handle this as you would any business transaction. Your business plan shows potential lenders how serious you are about making your business succeed and returning a profit as soon as possible.

The good thing about borrowing start-up capital from friends and family is that you can sweeten the pot by offering lenders a limited partnership, a percentage of profits, or other creative incentives. However, exercise caution when doing this, as you don't want to saddle yourself with a long-term business arrangement that may turn out to be less than ideal.

Crowdfunding

Crowdfunding is a relatively new concept, but it's catching on like wildfire. Simply put, crowdfunding is a collaborative internet platform where people can solicit financial backing from individuals willing to invest in a variety of causes and purposes. From political causes, to charities, to fundraisers, to medical emergencies, to business start-ups, people pitch their idea, business or cause to the masses in hopes that other people will donate money. In return, investors receive a token of appreciation - these can be T-shirts, posters, book dedications, thank you cards, or something specifically related to the "project".

Kickstarter, Gofundme and Indiegogo are probably the three most popular crowdfunding sites. Be sure to read all the details prior to listing your project. There are a few rules to follow and you want to be sure your project is a success.

Community Development Centers

Large and small communities all across the nation recognize the importance of fostering a sense of cooperative spirit. Community development centers and local chambers of commerce are excellent resources for small businesses. They can efficiently steer you in the right direction when seeking funding for your business. While they usually do not have the resources to lend money to entrepreneurs, they'll definitely know where you should go and who you should talk to.

Banks and Credit Unions

Make an appointment to discuss your business start-up options with your local bank or credit union loan officer. These people are financial experts with years of experience and they'll often gladly share their knowledge with you. This is where your business plan comes into play. If you've done your homework, your loan officer will see just how serious you are about your business. He or she will be happy to sit down and discuss your options.

Loan officers are professionals who will carefully comb over your business plan, current finances, expected start-up costs, projected profits and other pertinent information. They want to see you succeed almost as much as you do. If you don't understand something, ask for clarification. After learning of your loan options, carefully research these on your own as well. Financing your business via a bank loan is something to investigate vigilantly and thoroughly.

SBA Loans

The Small Business Administration (SBA) currently offers loans via the *Microloan Program*. These loans provide up to $50,000 to small businesses for start-up or expansion costs. According to the SBA, the average microloan is approximately $13,000. Microloans can be used for:

- Working capital
- Inventory
- Supplies
- Equipment
- Office furniture

Microloan repayment terms vary according to the loan amount, the needs of the borrower and other factors. For more information on microloans and the SBA, visit www.sba.gov.

Government Grants

This option isn't for the average entrepreneur, since the process can be extremely complex and regulations are rigorously adhered to. Certain business grants are available through state and local programs, non-profits and other groups. Generally, a business should pertain to a particular cause or specialized industry such as childcare, energy efficiency and technology, or tourism - things that benefit and assist individuals and communities. If your business fits into any of these categories, a government grant might be a viable option.

Grants are not always free money. Some grants require borrowers to match funds or subsidize grants with other types of loans. For more information on government grants, and for applications, you can visit www.grants.gov.

Venture Capital and Angel Investors

These are a type of equity financing and are made in exchange for shares and/or active roles in the company. Venture capital financing generally focuses on high-risk companies, with high growth potential and a high return on investment. Therefore, this type of financing is ideal for businesses that might have difficulty receiving financing from traditional sources, such as banks.

Venture capital is usually provided by wealthy investors (also known as angel investors) who recognize the potential for rapid growth in a business and are willing to take a financial risk. They remain actively involved in daily business operations - providing guidance, consultation, mentoring, and other valuable business advice.

Angel investors can be attorneys, doctors, dentists, professors, and other business professionals. Often, they are experienced entrepreneurs themselves. Venture capital financing can be a complex option, with positive, as well as negative, aspects. Research this financing option carefully before committing to working with an investor. To find a venture capital (or angel) investor start with people you know personally. Lawyers and accountants will often know people willing to invest in new businesses and can recommend them to you.

As you can see, you have many options when it comes to financing your business start-up. Fortunately for you, almost every one of the business ideas discussed in this book requires little to no funding, so you're most likely ready to proceed to the next step.

Insurance and Bonding

Whether we like it or not, we live in a litigious society. People often sue one another even for the slightest infraction. As a business owner, you may find it prudent to carry liability insurance. You may even find that some of your customers will insist that you be insured. Certain businesses are more risky than others, and therefore liability insurance is a wise investment.

Insurance protects businesses against liability issues and provides coverage for a variety of things. For example, if you own a housecleaning business and break an antique vase while cleaning, your insurance will pay the homeowner for their loss. Without insurance, you would be responsible for the cost of the broken vase. Several of the businesses outlined at the beginning of this book call for services to be performed in a client's home. For this reason alone, you should seriously consider carrying liability insurance. Insurance costs vary greatly and depend on the amount and type of coverage.

Bonding (also known as surety bonding) is similar to insuring, but differs slightly in that it protects the business owner on specific jobs. In the event that you perform a service for a client and they are unsatisfied with the results, or if the client accuses you of theft, a surety bond will pay out a claim. Bonding almost always involves a criminal background check. If you hire employees who will be working in clients' homes you should definitely discuss bonding options. Bonding is generally inexpensive, often as low as $50. This is an extremely cost effective marketing tool for almost any business.

Some companies opt for both surety bonding and insurance coverage. Talk to an insurance professional about your specific circumstances to be sure that you are properly covered, while taking care not to be over-insured, which can also be a costly mistake.

Keeping Records

If you don't already have a relationship with a professional accountant, now is the time to establish one. Knowledgeable CPAs have the expertise you need to set up a comprehensive bookkeeping system necessary for maintaining your business expenses and income. You may even opt to have your accountant perform all of your bookkeeping for you.

If you're trying to keep your expenses down to a minimum (and what small business owner isn't?) then you may wish to forgo a professional accountant in favor of setting up your own accounting system. A simple store-bought ledger can be used to keep track of your daily business transactions. A ledger is portable and light-weight, making it simple to transport wherever you go. You can easily glue an envelope to the back cover to store receipts until you have the opportunity to file them away.

Nowadays, everyone has a computer. Several spreadsheet and other accounting software programs are available online. If you have Word Office, then you have Excel. Excel is a powerful spreadsheet application. Many small business owners use Excel because it's easily customizable and there are additional templates available. As with any spreadsheet application software, there is a bit of a learning curve involved, but once you get the hang of it you'll appreciate the available bells and whistles - in particular the ability to create graphs and charts that enable you to compare income and expenditures at a glance. Your spreadsheet application software will do double and triple duty if you use it for scheduling and customer data entry in addition to recordkeeping purposes.

Whether you enter your records digitally or by hand, this is not a step you want to skip. Properly maintained financial records:

- Keep track of your business progress - Is your business making or losing money? Are you charging your customers too little or too much? Are your expenses too high?
- Identify any deductible expenses - There are many deductions available to small businesses. Keeping track of these will save you money in the long-run.

- Provide information necessary for tax preparation - You can eliminate the dreaded hunting and searching when April rolls around if your daily records are always kept up to date.
- Provide the IRS with any necessary information, should they ever request it.
- Demonstrate to investors and banks that your business is making money, should you eventually decide to expand your business and seek financing.

A good recordkeeping system is an invaluable business tool. It's satisfies IRS tax requirements and gives you an accurate picture of your business's financial health. This is definitely not a business aspect you want to ignore.

Daily Business Operations

Now that you've chosen a business, calculated your start-up costs, named and registered your business, decided on a business structure, chosen insurance or bonding (or both) and set up a comprehensive record keeping system you are ready to delve into the wonderful world of running your own business.

If you thought you weren't going to work as hard as you did while working for someone else you're sorely mistaken. Get ready to work harder than you ever have before. If you ditched the daily 9 to 5 grind because you thought you'd be working less hours, you're going to be disappointed. You'll probably work twice as many hours - at least in the beginning. So why would you be crazy enough to leave your job security in favor of going it alone if you'll be working twice as hard? Because:

1. You become your own boss
2. You have the ability to create jobs by hiring employees
3. You have unlimited earnings potential
4. You can create a more flexible work schedule
5. You establish something you can hand down to your children
6. You contribute to a cause you're passionate about
7. You can't be fired
8. You personally profit from all your effort
9. You can work in your pajamas if you like
10. You can commute to your living room
11. You keep your mind active and sharp
12. You operate under your own morals and values, not someone else's
13. You are continuously challenging yourself creatively
14. You get paid to do something you love
15. You choose who you work with

There are many more advantages than there are disadvantages to being your own boss. You already know this, or you wouldn't be reading this book. While there's no denying operating a business is hard work, the rewards far outweigh the difficulties. The next few sections address and attempt to prevent any foreseeable issues, problems and concerns you may have while operating your business. Some firsthand knowledge, tips and techniques of daily operations are included.

Setting up Shop

Almost every business mentioned at the beginning of this book qualifies as an ideal home based business. Operating out of your home saves a small fortune in overhead costs. Think of all the money you'll save on rent, utilities, property insurance and other expenses. Furthermore, if you're as fastidious with your record and tax keeping duties as you should be, you can deduct some of your operating expenses from your income tax. Be sure to consult with a tax professional before doing this, however. Saving money on transportation costs is an additional benefit. Commuting to your living room in your pajamas is certainly an undeniable plus.

You may be fortunate enough to require very little space to run your business. Much of many service business activities are carried out in customers' homes. A corner of your bedroom or your kitchen table may be all that's needed to schedule appointments, contact customers, record daily transactions and order supplies. Operating materials, if kept to a minimum, can be stored in your garage or even a closet.

There are tons of home office ideas online. *Pinterest* has hundreds of inspirational photos available. Browse online, and in brick and mortar storage retailers to discover clever options. DIY websites offer suggestions for manufacturing your own storage solutions - making your own work desk, shelving and storage bins from recycled wood, crates and baskets is far less expensive than purchasing ready-made storage items. One word of advice, however, if your business requires you to sit for long hours at a desk, you'll want to invest in a good ergonomic chair.

Buy Used

In your excitement to get your new business up and going you may be tempted to rush to buy everything new. For example, if you've opted to start a home daycare, you'll probably need child-size furniture, bookshelves, books, toys, sleep mats, etc. Before purchasing new and expensive items, consider buying gently used goods. Resale shops exist in every corner of the country and these can be excellent resources for small business owners. Search classified ads, as well, to find moneysaving deals. Regardless of the business, almost any type of equipment is available secondhand. Keep an eye on local auctions, business liquidation sales, and scratch and dent deals. Check to see if a local chapter of FreeCycle.org exists in your area. You could potentially save hundreds of dollars by buying used items.

Save Money on Supplies

The same thing goes for your daily supplies. Many new business owners are quick to purchase more supplies than they actually need. Not only is this expensive, you have to find a place to store everything. Make a list of the materials you absolutely need at start-up and carefully stick to your list.

In the beginning, you may find that purchasing the bulk of your supplies from local supercenters and warehouse stores works for you. You can find some great deals when shopping at these outlets. You should keep an eye out for sale items listed in retail flyers. Clipping coupons can also save you money on everyday items. Eventually, however, you may find that you can save money by buying in bulk via wholesalers.

Working with Wholesalers

As with most information nowadays, the internet is an excellent place to start when searching for wholesale suppliers. Simply type in _____ wholesalers (fill in the blank with your particular wholesale supply needs). Make a list of possible sites to visit. Be sure to verify the following, since these considerations will affect your final costs:

- What (if any) are the minimum order requirements?
- How much are the shipping costs?
- What bulk discounts are offered?
- How quickly are orders shipped?

If your business sells products to customers you should check for wholesalers who offer drop ship options. You can save a lot of money by having items shipped directly to your customers. Many drop shippers will include a shipping label with your business name and info so that customers only see your information.

Wholesalers can save small businesses time and money - time and money better spent on other aspects of business operations. However, since you might be investing a sizeable amount of money to meet minimum order requirements you should do your homework to be sure you're dealing with reputable, reliable wholesalers. Check with the Better Business Bureau (BBB) to see if a wholesaler has any complaints filed.

One thing to note: If you find wholesale minimum order requirements to be cost prohibitive, consider collaborating with friends, family and/or other small business owners to pool your orders. This is a great way to lower your supply costs.

If your business includes the sale of products be aware that most states require that you obtain a *State Sales Tax Number* or *Resale Certificate.* You will be required to collect sales tax from your customers, and then the collected tax must be paid to your state. Depending upon your type of business and the amount of your revenue, you will then be required to report the collected tax either monthly or quarterly.

Most wholesalers require you to provide a state sales tax number prior to placing your initial order. With this sales tax number, you are able to purchase items without paying sales tax. Items purchased with a sales tax number via wholesaler must be for resale or for qualified business use.

For more information on applying for a sales tax number contact your State Department of Revenue. You can usually do this online. Your local Chamber of Commerce can also be a valuable resource for advice when applying for a resale certificate.

Dealing with Difficult Customers

At some time during your entrepreneurial journey you will undoubtedly come across an unhappy, angry or just plain dissatisfied customer. Remember how you were asked to assess your *soft skills* at the beginning of this book? You were asked if you were a *people person*. This is when your answers will be put to the test.

Reputation is everything in business. Word of mouth will probably be your biggest marketing tool. A satisfied customer has the potential to bring you dozens of new clients - at no cost to you. On the flipside, a dissatisfied customer can cause a lot of damage and cost you revenue in the process. Even more so than making money, keeping customers happy should be your main goal. Without happy customers you will soon find yourself out of business. How do you deal with a dissatisfied customer?

- First, stop what you're doing and truly listen to what your customer is saying. If you take a step back and view the situation from the client's perspective you should be able to resist the temptation to go on the offensive. Do this by listening attentively without interrupting and without formulating an immediate response (you can't truly listen to someone if you're mentally preparing your response).
- Mirror, or repeat, the customer's concerns so you're both on the same page. Ask questions for clarification if necessary. Use a calming tone without sounding condescending. A calm, composed response will almost always diffuse the situation.
- Apologize for the poor service or product. Ask the customer how they would like the problem remedied. Offer solutions to the problem. This can be the suggestion of a refund or exchange.
- Put yourself in the customer's shoes. Think about the last time you were unhappy with the products or services you received. What did you hope to gain from voicing your concerns?
- Look at the situation as an opportunity to improve your business. Successful companies want positive, as well as negative, input from customers. You may not even know a problem exists until a customer brings it to your attention.
- Follow up by calling or visiting the customer. Be sure the problem has been resolved and the customer is satisfied with the resolution.

Sometimes you will come across a customer who is determined to be unhappy regardless of the solution you present. You may even encounter a verbally abusive customer. Determining ahead of time what kinds of behavior you will or will not personally tolerate should prepare you for this scenario. As much as you might hate losing a customer, terminating an abusive business relationship may be your only recourse.

Hiring Employees or Independent Contractors

At some point you may find yourself so swamped with clients and overwhelmed with work that you may consider hiring employees or independent contractors. Think long and hard before hiring *employees* because:

- You are responsible for your employees' actions and behavior while they are conducting business on your behalf
- You are legally required to withhold taxes, pay benefits, and carry state unemployment and worker's compensation insurance
- You must pay employees whether you have work for them or not
- Training and turnover can be expensive

Working with an independent contractor (IC) can be a more cost-effective, beneficial alternative to hiring employees. ICs:

- Are paid only for the work provided, on a per-contract basis
- Provide their own tools and equipment
- Employ and pay their own employees
- Operate under their own business name
- Keep their own financial and other records

All is not sunshine and roses when working with ICs, however. Unlike with employees, you will not have the control over the quality of work you may desire because you won't have the same level of supervision you'd have over an employee. In addition, since you are not required to maintain worker's comp insurance for an IC, you'd better make darn sure they have their own liability and/or accident insurance since you might very well be responsible for damages or injuries incurred during a job performed on your behalf. You should consult an insurance agent to see what additional insurance options are available to businesses that contract with independents.

According to the SBA, *"Whether a person is an independent contractor or an employee generally depends on the amount of control exercised by the employer over the work being done."* If you are uncertain whether to hire an employee or an independent contractor, or if you've already hired someone and want to be sure you are operating legally under required laws you should speak to a tax professional or visit the IRS website for more information on specific guidelines. Misclassification of workers can be an expensive mistake.

Marketing and Advertising Your Business

After all the time and effort you've spent conceptualizing, creating, preparing, organizing, calculating, registering, formulating and planning - not to mention the money you may have spent - it's time to let people know about your new business venture. Operating a business without marketing and advertising it is like planning a party and forgetting to send out the invitations. No one will show up if you neglect this vital step. A carefully planned marketing strategy is critical to the success of your business.

Although many people use the terms marketing and advertising interchangeably, there is a distinct difference. Simply put, marketing is the creation and formulation of ideas in order to *brand* a person or business. It includes researching your target market to find the best plan to reach specific customers. It is the *big picture* and the *whole process* conceptualized when attempting to attract *consumers* and convert them into *customers*.

Advertising is part of marketing in that it is the *paid communications and promotions* of a business, product or individual. Think newspaper ads, classifieds, business cards, press releases, radio and television ads, etc.

In the past, experts have estimated that 1/3 of a business's revenue should be spent on marketing and advertising. Nowadays, that may not necessarily be the case. There are so many free and low-cost options that every small and large business owner should be accessing. The internet and social media in particular have opened a world of opportunities for businesses to brand themselves, and many of these opportunities are FREE.

Regardless of how much you allocate towards your marketing and advertising campaign, it's important not to think of marketing in terms of cost, but rather as an *investment* in your company. Every single marketing tool or technique you utilize in business should produce a profitable *return on investment* (ROI) or it's not doing you any good and you need to find a new marketing method. If you're *investing* your valuable time and money in a particular marketing strategy, you should expect to see an increase in sales and/or customers. Otherwise why would you do it? Simple. This is an extremely important piece of information and you should keep this in mind at all times.

In order to plan a successful marketing strategy you'll need to find out who your potential customers are by conducting a bit of *market research*. It can be a costly mistake to target the wrong market. For example, if your business manufactures and sells gourmet dog biscuits you'd be wasting your time and money advertising in a woodworking magazine or setting up a booth at a gun show (I know it sounds ridiculous, but you might be surprised at the mistakes some new entrepreneurs make). Market research can be as simple as creating and distributing brief questionnaires. As an example, if you're marketing your apartment cleaning business, you could develop a brief questionnaire asking potential customers:

- How satisfied they are with their current cleaning company
- How much they'd be willing to spend on weekly apartment cleaning
- What services are most important to them
- What day of the week is most convenient for them

You could then ask rental offices for permission to leave your questionnaires with them or ask to hang them on a community bulletin board. The information gained from questionnaires can be a valuable resource when determining who your target market is and how best to serve them.

There are many things home based and small businesses should be doing to attract new customers and to keep existing ones. Marketing and advertising is a never-ending process for small business owners, but that doesn't mean it has to cost you thousands, or even hundreds, of dollars. I've included some excellent, proven methods to secure clients and keep them. Many of these methods are low-cost and even free.

Branding

Competition in business is fierce. Everyone is clamoring for a piece of the pie and it's vital to your business's success that you continually stay in the spotlight. Positioning yourself as an expert in your chosen field, and then constantly proving it, will attract a steady supply of customers and help keep the ones you already have. Successfully branding your business is designed to set you apart from your competitors. An effective brand strategy should tell consumers who you are, what you offer and why they should choose your business over others like it. Are you an apartment cleaner who gets the job done in record time, at minimal cost? Are you a personal trainer who offers a low-cost, highly effective fitness routine that anyone can squeeze into their busy day? These are both examples of branding.

Defining your brand is the first step in your marketing strategy. To do this, make a list of the following:

- What does your company stand for?
- Who are your customers?
- How does your company differ from your competitors?
- What image will you convey to customers?
- What are your personal and business philosophies?

The answers to these questions will be the basis of your *Mission Statement*.

Mission Statement

Your Mission Statement is a critical first step in branding your business. Practically anyone can start their own business. However, if you don't have a well-defined statement that succinctly states what your business is about it will be difficult to convey this message to your customers, suppliers, and potential employees as clearly as necessary. A Mission Statement is as important as your business plan, but is not nearly as long. By taking the answers to the above questions and constructing your Mission Statement you will help to define and clarify the motivations for your business. This process is beneficial for your customers, as well as for you. If done correctly, it's an additional step in your journey of entrepreneurial self-discovery.

As stated, a Mission Statement is a short, concise declaration - usually no more than a paragraph or two. Search online examples to get an idea of what other companies include in their statements. Brainstorm with partners, friends and family to get a variety of perspectives.

Your Mission Statement deserves a prominent place in your workspace, where you and your associates will see it on a daily basis. It should also live on its own page on your website. Having it printed on your brochures and other correspondence is also advised.

Slogan

You may or may not decide to come up with a slogan for your business. A well-crafted slogan is an excellent complementary tagline to accompany your logo and other professional content. It should be a brief, promotional statement telling consumers what your company represents. The best company slogans are catchy, attention-getting and memorable. Think of all the slogans you're familiar with - *Where's the beef?*®, *Finger lickin' good*®, *Snap, Crackle Pop*®, *Because you're worth it*®, *Just do it*® - you're probably familiar with all of these, and you probably know the products they represent: *Wendy's, Kentucky Fried Chicken, Rice Krispies, L'Oreal and Nike* respectively. Slogans are fantastic marketing tools for any business.

Some slogans are funny, some impart factual information, some are flashy and hip, and some are old-fashioned and *homey*. However, they all have two things in common: They're *one sentence long* and they're *simple*. You might understand certain technical aspects of your business, but your potential customers probably won't. Don't confuse them with technical jargon. The best slogans entertain (aka are *funny*) and inform.

Thinking about the product or service you're selling will help determine which tactic to take. Write down a few ideas and try them out on friends and family. If you feel that writing isn't exactly your forte, ask talented writer friends for help. You can also find freelance writers who specialize in slogan writing.

Logo

Just like your slogan, your company logo should be an accurate representation of your company. Developing an attractive logo that truly reflects you and your business is a critical first step in the branding process. Designing a logo is not something to be taken lightly. You'll probably go through several revisions before getting it as near perfect as possible.

If you are artistically inclined you may wish to tackle this yourself. Start with a preliminary sketch or go straight to your computer. You can use PhotoShop, Gimp or even PowerPoint, the last of which is often overlooked, underutilized and underappreciated.

Refer to your slogan, as this might be a natural jumping off point. Incorporating a slogan into a logo works nicely. Logos can simply be words or words combined with graphics. Custom fonts are available online. Check out Google Fonts for downloads. Positioning a custom font alongside or within an attractive graphic can be a powerfully motivating logo.

If you decide to have a logo designed for you, consider asking artistic friends and family first. This can save you quite a bit of money. Expect to pay anywhere from $100 on the low end for a run of the mill logo, to thousands of dollars for a high quality design.

Elevator Pitch

Think of your *Elevator Pitch* (aka *Elevator Speech*) as a variation of your Mission Statement. In other words, if you were limited to the time spent during one elevator ride how would you describe your business?

When giving your pitch to potential customers you should answer the following three questions:

1. What is your product or service?
2. Why are you the best man or woman for the job?
3. Who are your competitors, and what makes you better than them?

When giving your pitch to potential investors you will need to address these two additional questions:

1. Who is your target market?
2. How will you make money?

Opening your pitch with a compelling hook is an excellent way to grab your listener's immediate attention. A persuasive fact that pertains to your business will make listeners want to hear more. However, be careful not to drone on while stating dry facts for several minutes. Ideally, your pitch should not last longer than 60 seconds and be no more than 150 - 200 words (225 is okay, but that's pushing it). Remember to allow your enthusiasm to come across in your pitch. Speaking passionately shows you're excited and positive about your endeavor. Finally, your pitch should end with a call to action. Extend an offer to schedule a presentation, meeting or other follow-up appointment. Practice your pitch on friends and family. Ask them for opinions, comments and suggestions.

Websites

With determination, hard work and a bit of luck you'll have a steady stream of clients. You may even begin to wish you could work 7 days a week, 24 hours a day for a chance to turn potential clients into satisfied, repeat customers. Unfortunately, you have to eat, sleep and attend to personal obligations. If only there was a place that continuously attracts, entertains, educates and persuades new customers. Well, guess what? There is and it's your very own website!

Gone are the days where you had to pay a webmaster to create your website from the ground up. Many businesses are recognizing the benefits of using *WordPress.com* and *Blogger*. What once began as blogging platforms, WordPress.com and Blogger.com sites can be easily customized and transformed into company websites. What's great about WordPress.com (not *WordPress.org*) and Blogger is that they are both free to use. They both offer a large variety of templates and other customizations so you can create a website that stands out over others. They do have their limitations, however, and you may find yourself eventually looking for alternatives.

Operating your website on the powerful *WordPress.org* platform is an excellent, cost-effective alternative. With the WordPress *Content Management System* (CMS) you have many more template, plug-in, widget and other really cool options you don't have with a website hosted on WordPress.com or Blogger. There are no annoying advertisements (unless you decide to place them on your site to earn revenue) like you have with Blogger and WordPress.com. And, the best thing is you don't need to know a lick of HTML. This makes it possible for the average person to add content, photos, forms, polls and other important marketing elements anytime they like, quickly and easily.

If you're not interested in a WordPress.org website (frankly, why wouldn't you be?), you can find other free website builders on the internet, but these look less professional since they usually have the website builder's name displayed prominently somewhere on your website (who wants that?). You can also pay someone to design a website for you, but that comes with a hefty price tag. You'll also need to know html in order to change, add or delete content, otherwise you'll be paying additional fees to your webmaster to do this on your behalf. Whichever you choose, make sure you choose something. A website is an absolute necessity in business nowadays. It's a powerful marketing tool that keeps working even when you're not.

Blogs

Contrary to what many people believe, a *blog* is not the same thing as a business website. Blogs operate on a more informal, personal level. This is where you include articles, daily or weekly updates, and other content related to your area of expertise. It's also acceptable to include a bit about yourself as an individual, separate from your business. It gives your readers (aka potential and existing customers) the opportunity to interact with you in a casual setting via comments. Additionally, whenever you write content on your blog you should most definitely share it via a variety of social media platforms. This has the huge benefit of positioning you as an expert in your field. It opens the door to an even greater customer base.

Your blog should be frequently updated, to keep visitors coming back for more. Blogs can include giveaways and coupons (more on these later), discount information, photos and other motivational content, all of which can be included and cross-posted to your website. Remember to invite questions and comments to keep readers interested and engaged.

Be sure to link to your business website from your blog and vice versa. Your main goal is to convert visitors into customers. Don't ever forget, this is always your most important objective when maintaining a blog.

Newsletters

Newsletters are additional opportunities to engage and convert readers into customers. Most marketing experts agree that company newsletters almost always produce a high rate of ROI (return on investment), which means the time and money you spend designing, preparing and emailing your newsletter will almost certainly net you a profitable ROI in terms of sales and/or new customers.

Whether you write and distribute your own newsletter or turn that responsibility over to a professional you can expect to increase your customer base by doing so. While you can certainly go to the expense of printing hardcopies of your newsletter and mailing them, emailing newsletters to subscribers is far more preferable and cost-effective.

Place newsletter signup forms on your company website and your blog. Never, ever send newsletters to people who have not formally signed up to receive them - that's spamming and it's a definite no-no. Spending your valuable time marketing your newsletter to people who actually want to read it is much wiser anyway.

Using email and newsletter marketing companies like *MailChimp* and *Constant Contact* to create eye-catching newsletters, while also keeping track of subscribers, will simplify the process. Additionally, using these services and others like them will make your newsletters look professional and polished.

Most companies email newsletters on a monthly basis. Some companies limit their newsletters to quarterlies. The frequency you decide on will depend upon how much information you have to share.

Newsletters generally include a brief representation of the content you've published on your website or blog over the previous month. Things like photos, articles, blog posts, videos, in the form of website links, are all ideal subject matter for your monthly newsletter. Newsletters are designed to engage, entertain and build a sense of loyalty and commitment between you and your clients. What's important to remember when preparing your newsletter is to avoid writing one long advertisement. . In other words, your newsletter should contain more valuable information for readers than it does promotional advertising for your company. Screaming *buy this, buy that* will get your newsletter tossed in the trash and your subscribers will promptly unsubscribe. Instead, your customers will find greater value in your newsletter if you include lots of useful information such as tips, advice, industry secrets, and other things to help readers. Don't forget to add snippets of positive reviews and comments from satisfied customers. Coupons and discount codes are also an acceptable element to include in newsletters. Reserve the sales pitch for your email marketing campaigns.

Email Marketing

Some people think email marketing is dead or at least dying, but this is simply untrue. The recent resurgence of promotional email strategies is proof-positive that email marketing works. Over 90% of online consumers have given companies permission to send them promotional information via email. Additionally, 75% of online consumers state they prefer receiving promotional advertising via email. If you think about it, this makes sense since many consumers are becoming increasingly aware of the true costs of print advertising. Consider this:

- The average household receives 5 or more pieces of junk mail each day
- Junk mail accounts for 1 billion pounds of garbage in our landfills every year
- The U.S. produces enough junk mail in just 5 days to reach the moon
- 2.6 Million trees are destroyed every year to create junk mail

Pay particular attention to how much junk mail ends up in our landfills each year. Not only is this an enormous contribution to our ever-growing waste-management issues, it shows how ineffective it is to randomly distribute unsolicited print advertisements. Emailing promotional content to consumers who've specifically requested it is a much better solution. In fact, response rates for email marketing range from 5% to 35%, while response rates for printed direct mail barely add up to 3%. This translates into a higher rate of ROI.

For email marketing to be effective, you need viable leads. Do not purchase mailing lists - this is a waste of time and money. Do you remember that newsletter signup form you placed on your blog and website? You now have the opportunity to send promotional and/or monthly emails to anyone who has signed up via that form. Just don't overdo the promotional emails. No one likes to be bombarded with daily emails touting the latest sales, announcements, etc. Do this sparingly and to announce things like a new product or service, exclusive deal or special event.

You can construct a specifically designed signup form to gain as much information about your leads (potential customers) as you like. Knowing details such as geographical area, age, likes, dislikes and other pertinent information allows you to better understand your customers. It also gives you the opportunity to customize your products and services to best suit their wants and needs.

The main goal to any effective email campaign is to *convert email subscribers into customers*. A successful email marketing promotion should always:

1. Drive subscribers to visit your website (where they can make a purchase)
2. Motivate subscribers to take some type of immediate action by purchasing your product or service

Mobile Marketing

Let's all admit it - we're in love with our mobile phones. We carry them everywhere and check them repeatedly throughout the day. Chances are, as you're sitting here reading this book, your beloved phone isn't far out of your reach, ready to be grabbed the minute you hear it ring, ding or sing. This is why mobile marketing is capturing the attention of companies looking for new and effective ways of marketing their goods and services to consumers.

So what is mobile marketing? Simply put, it's marketing your business via mobile text messages. If you've downloaded a QR code app to your phone and used it to access a company website you've experienced mobile marketing. Or, if you play games on your smartphone and those pesky (or intriguing) ads pop up in between sets you've also been part of a marketing campaign. Companies know this is a quick, easy and effective method of marketing their businesses to consumers.

As a new small business owner, you probably won't have the big bucks it takes to run a large scale mobile marketing campaign. There are also many rules and regulations to follow when marketing via mobile phones. There are short code considerations, as well as compliance issues - more than we can possibly go into in this book. Therefore, mobile marketing is a method best left to experts. However, you can easily include a QR code on your advertising literature to make it convenient for consumers to visit your website to find out more about you and your business. There are many free QR code generator websites where you can easily create the code to place on your advertising materials. Qrstuff.com is an excellent one-stop website for this purpose.

Business Resume

You may think that resumes are just for job candidates who are currently in the job market. However, a professional resume is the ideal document for the small business owner. A resume that includes your expertise, education, and work and personal experience can be easily distributed to potential clients, professional organizations you may wish to join, conference and exhibition organizers, and agencies handling bids on major projects.

Follow the general rules of resume writing by:

- Placing your contact information at the top
- Limit your business resume to no more than two pages
- Use standard font (Times New Roman is the standard)
- Use bullets whenever possible to make it simple to read
- Be concise and specific

Word includes several resume templates and there are many more available for free download on the Microsoft website. Check out sample resumes online to get an idea of how your business resume should look.

Your business resume can easily be saved as a PDF file where it can live on its own page on your website if you like. Networking websites like *LinkedIn* make it simple to upload your resume online. Take advantage of this feature as it can often result in additional sales. An online resume is the perfect marketing tool that requires little attention aside from the occasional update.

Social Media

Many of us already have Facebook and Twitter accounts. When it comes to social media, these are the two biggies. However, you do not want to mix business with pleasure when it comes to social media. You'll want to register accounts across all social media platforms and designate these solely for your business. This means every tweet and post needs to be strictly related to your business, area of expertise or industry. Occasionally sharing something personal is usually acceptable, but before you do you need to ask yourself how it will reflect on you as a business owner. Will it be a negative or positive reflection? Other than that, stick to business. Talking about what you ate for lunch and how you hate the government will not further your efforts to brand yourself as an expert in your field.

LinkedIn is an excellent professional networking platform that every business owner should be using. Connecting and engaging with likeminded individuals and organizations can establish you as an expert in your field. Joining LinkedIn groups provides the opportunity to connect even further. Enter your particular field or industry into the LinkedIn search bar and this will yield hundreds of possibilities. Be sure to visit your groups periodically and contribute to discussions and threads so people will get to know you. Ask and answer questions and you'll soon become the go-to person in the group.

Facebook pages are simple to create. All you need is a personal account first and then you're able to add *pages* from there. Fill in your business information carefully. You have the opportunity to include a short description as well as a longer description. Be sure to have the link to your website front and center. Take advantage of the *tabs*. There are tons of applications to include in your tabs. Make a contact form one of them so visitors can easily get in touch with you.

Pinterest is the up and coming leader in social media - particularly when it comes to generating leads for retailers. Photo-driven, Pinterest is a fantastic way for retailers to advertise their goods online. If you sell a product you should definitely register a business account (this gives Pinterest visitors the ability to click straight through to your website) and download the Pinterest app to your phone for on-the-go accessibility.

Don't make the mistake that many newbie social media users do. It is definitely not all about you. The quickest ways to get unfollowed or unliked is to:

- Scream "buy my product or service" in every other tweet or post
- Ignore your followers
- Be overly self-promotional
- Post a succession of links only
- Post photos only

Instead, be sure to engage your followers with posts that include valuable and helpful information. People want to know how *you* can help *them*. If your tweets and posts contain useful tips, advice and other practical content you will gain and retain more followers while positioning yourself as an expert in your field. Again, it's all about branding.

So, what should you, as a small business owner, be tweeting and posting? Make a point of seeking out valuable articles, how-to tips and advice from experts to share via social media. Remember that blog you started? Write and publish some great posts and share them. In fact, every time you post something to your blog, you should immediately share it via social media. Besides Twitter and Facebook, you should know about several others:

- Digg
- Reddit
- StumbleUpon
- Tumblr
- Google+
- LinkedIn
- Pinterest
- Pocket

With social media it's all about schmoozing. It's about walking that fine line between engaging with customers and other business owners, while gently and subtly marketing your business. However, don't spend so much time on social media that you end up ignoring your business duties. No one expects you to sit at your computer all day and night tweeting and posting your pearls of wisdom. Sign up for a free *Hootsuite* or another social media management service and schedule your tweets and posts ahead of time.

Finally, keep in mind that it's not all about numbers. It's more about the value of each of your followers. You do not have to follow everyone who follows you. Spend your time connecting with people in your industry and those who can help you get your business message out to consumers. Don't forget to return the favor. People are more likely to go the extra mile for those who are quick to reciprocate by retweeting and reposting.

Press Release

No, the press release is not dead. It's very much alive, ready and willing to help you market your business to literally thousands of possible clients. That doesn't mean you should automatically write (or pay someone to write) a press release. Your press release needs to be *newsworthy* first. This means it should focus on a specific event. For example:

- A grand opening
- Website launch
- New product
- New service
- Special sale

There are other occasions where a press release is appropriate. The key is being creative and *spinning* your amazing news into a succinct, informative report that will be sure to capture the attention of readers. There are specific elements to keep in mind when writing a press release. These are:

- Contact information: Your name, email address and Web URL are a must. You might also wish to add your business address and phone number.
- Capture attention with a headline: All boldfaced caps, short, action-packed, with a clear benefit to your reader.
- Make the initial 10 words really count: Your opening sentence is critical. An attention-grabbing *hook* will pique your readers' interest.
- Why should people care about what you have to say?: Consumers want to know what's in it for them. Concentrating on how they will benefit from using your product or service guarantees they will read to the end.
- Just the facts, ma'am: Don't waste space with superfluous or fancy words. State pertinent facts as succinctly and factually as possible. And while you're at it, avoid any technical jargon.

- Add a quote or two: A quote from a satisfied customer and a quote from you as the business owner adds credibility to your press release.
- Add cost information: This works better for products, since this probably won't vary. The cost of services can sometimes fluctuate. You might not always wish to divulge your pricing. A general cost or price point might be more appropriate in some cases.
- Repeat your contact information at the end: Make it super simple for people to get in touch with you.

Don't forget to proofread and edit your press release for proper grammar and spelling. Have someone else read it for you to catch any mistakes you may have missed. Next, share your press release via:

- Free and paid online press release submission sites
- Local television and radio stations
- Local newspapers
- Your website and blog
- Social media websites

If in doubt about who and where to submit hard copies of your press release, be sure to call ahead and find out. This will ensure that your press release ends up on the appropriate desk. With a little bit of work you can craft a compelling press release that will result in potential business leads.

Seminars, Workshops and Webinars

Seminars and workshops are excellent platforms to utilize when looking to position yourself as a professional in your chosen field. You've chosen to operate a business because you're passionate about what you do and you've found a viable way to make money while doing it. Take that passion and channel it into seminars, workshops and webinars.

Your main goal with this marketing method is not making money (although that could be an added plus), your goal is to acquire as many new customers as possible. However, you need to walk the fine line between selling and educating. Participants must be convinced that attending your event will result in their receiving something valuable in return - whether it be free information, complimentary products, discount offers or other useful goods or service. Otherwise they won't be willing to attend. If you've ever been lured into attending an event that was clearly a longwinded sales pitch and felt cheated at the end you'll understand. This *freebie* will be your *hook* to entice people to register for your event.

When planning your seminar, workshop or webinar you'll want to be sure it's a balanced mix of unique information, visual aids and interactive activities, such as:

- Infographics
- Slideshows
- Videos
- PowerPoint presentations
- Handouts
- Booklets
- Questionnaires
- Q&A sessions

These elements have the ability to entertain *and* inform your participants. A huge amount of information can be packed into any of these visual components.

You want your students to be hungry for the information you have to share with them. However, don't give them the whole meal - you just want to give people a taste of what's to come. Remember, these seminars, workshops and webinars are ultimately designed as *marketing tools*. They should be intended solely to turn your participants into clients. The conclusion should include your contact info and purchase links.

Your workshops can be given at local schools, churches, libraries or in your home. They're excellent for hands-on activities. For example, if your business is making and selling hand knit baby items, you could consider offering a workshop on knitting newborn caps. This has the advantage of teaching students a valuable skill, while offering the opportunity to purchase your handcrafted items. If you've chosen to operate a pet sitting business you could give a workshop on pet massage. Being creative will result in a variety of workshop ideas.

Seminars often rely heavily on lecture, visuals and print content. They're ideal vehicles for service-related businesses. For instance, if you're a graphics designer you could give a seminar on the importance of creating an eye-catching website. If your business is house sitting, your seminar could be geared towards home safety tips and advice. The possibilities are almost endless.

Online *webinars* teach participants a new skill, technique or method and have the potential of reaching many more people than you would when teaching in a classroom setting. The internet has made it possible to connect with likeminded people all over the world. Instructing students in the comfort of their own homes (and yours) is becoming more and more popular because of the convenience factor. There are several online webinar and meeting services available, making it simple to register an account and begin scheduling online trainings. The great thing about hosting webinars is, once recorded, you can grab the code and embed it on your website to be watched by thousands of additional viewers. You can also share the recording via social media. It truly becomes a marketing tool that keeps working for you long after it has originally aired.

Whether you choose to host seminars, workshops, webinars, or a combination of all three, keep in mind that your ultimate goal is *turning attendees into clients*!

If you don't wish to sponsor your own workshop, seminar or webinar you should definitely consider volunteering or getting paid to do guest speaking engagements. Many non-profit and for-profit companies and organizations actively book professionals to speak at meetings, conventions and other events. As an example, with a house sitting business, your home safety seminar would be highly suitable for local women's groups, home owners associations and community watch groups wishing to book event speakers.

Print Marketing

Although the internet has practically taken complete control over our marketing (and basically our lives) the humble business card and other print advertising is still working hard for business owners. Far less costly than having a website built, print marketing materials can literally cost pennies and continue working for you long after they leave your hands.

Print marketing materials can include:

- Business cards
- Business stationery
- Brochures
- Flyers
- Pamphlets
- Postcards
- Posters
- Magnetic signs for vehicles
- Direct mailings
- Promotional products (T-shirts, key chains, pens, etc.)

It's the little things that count and have the potential to attract more business in the process. Adding a notice of a special promo with your invoices will certainly catch the attention of your existing customers. For example, you can slip a "tell a friend and receive 10% off your next order" card in with an invoice. In fact, including almost any of the above materials with your invoices is attention-getting marketing.

Video Trailer Marketing

Movie studios have been doing this for decades. How many times have you sat through several movie trailers while waiting for a feature film to begin? How many times have you decided to see a movie simply because a movie trailer caught your attention and lured you in? Trailer marketing works! It encapsulates an entire movie by using the most exciting, compelling scenes and sums it up in just a few minutes. Why shouldn't you be doing this with your business?

YouTube is BIG business and you should be riding its coattails when promoting *your* business. Thousands of videos are uploaded to YouTube daily. It's fast, simple and FREE.

According to a recent Nielsen report, the spending power of today's American consumer is continually increasing and tops well over $25 trillion per year. Consumers also spend a great deal of time online. Women watch an average of 191:34 hours of video each month, which is up significantly from previous years. Studies show that women are more active online than men. Regardless of the type of product or service you sell, you should be including video marketing in your advertising portfolio. But, if your business caters to women, you have even more reason to market via video trailers. Advertising and marketing via videos is still an often-overlooked concept for businesses, but it shouldn't be.

Most consumers have short attention spans. They want to know what's in it for them. Summing up your product or service in a couple of minutes or less ensures you'll capture the attention of targeted consumers and keep it.

A well-designed and effective video doesn't have to be long. In fact, a minute to two minutes is ideal and all you need to get your business message across to existing and potential customers. Video marketing is a suitable tool for any business – regardless of service or product.

As an example, the video book trailer has become an excellent marketing tool for authors. Indie authors, in particular, have come to appreciate the effectiveness of using this advertising vehicle on their websites and social media posts. YouTube makes it simple to copy, share and embed code practically anywhere. There's no reason why video marketing can't also be utilized by big and small businesses.

The cost for video trailers vary, but are quite affordable and are available for any budget. The average business owner can tackle Windows Movie Maker themselves. If you don't already have this program on your computer, you can quickly and safely download it from Microsoft.com. The impact video trailers make with consumers is definitely worth the effort.

Volunteer

Volunteering your services at local organizations and charitable facilities will get your name out into the community. Also known as *charity marketing*, smart business owners recognize how beneficial this process is to everyone. Developing and growing your business by connecting with members of your community while helping them is a rewarding undertaking. It can also result in dozens of new customers for you.

Deciding where, how and when to volunteer your services is important. Choose organizations that you're passionate about - your passion will come across in your work. Charities that involve your target market would be the most natural fit. For example, if your business is pet sitting, volunteering to help with SPCA fundraisers would work nicely.

Never miss an opportunity to publicize your volunteer events. There's absolutely nothing wrong with this. Charities understand that ultimately you're a business person, trying to build your company. They accept this, since you're providing a valuable service and you'll most likely be advertising the event for them. When performing charity marketing be sure to:

- Write and distribute a press release detailing the charitable event.
- Add your charity work to your business resume and portfolio.
- Include your work with charitable organizations on brochures, pamphlets, websites, etc.
- Ask the charity if they'd consider including you and your volunteer work on some of their marketing materials (only

do this after you've fully established yourself with the charity).

To find charities and non-profits interested in your volunteer services simply call and ask. Most of these organizations are understaffed and underfunded, and are happy to have the additional assistance.

Be sure to find an appropriate balance between volunteer and paid work. While it's admirable to help your community while marketing your business, your main priority should be increasing profits. Before accepting volunteer opportunities ask yourself if the arrangement will be beneficial to all parties involved.

Write

As a business owner, you should be utilizing every free marketing opportunity available to you. This should include writing opportunities. If you have a way with words, writing can be an excellent FREE marketing tool. Do you remember the previous section on *branding*? Promoting your business via online articles gives you the opportunity to share your bio, website and other pertinent links that will direct people to places where they can find out more about you. Many freelance writers avoid so-called content mills because they pay little to nothing for a writer's efforts. However, your goal with this marketing tool is to communicate your expertise and knowledge in your articles, while driving traffic to your company website. That's an effort that can potentially secure dozens of new clients for your business.

Search online article sites. Some sites require that you submit a sample and wait for approval before you can begin contributing articles. Other sites simply ask that you register with the site and then you're free to submit articles. Search online article sites to find the right fit for you. Use the *profile section* wisely, since this is a representation of you and your business.

Guest blogging is also a good way to share information about yourself, your business and your area of expertise. Bloggers often actively seek guests to post content. It's difficult to come up with a steady supply of blog posts. Guest bloggers provide a break for blog owners. Search online blogs that center around your business. Contact the blog owner and offer to contribute a guest post. Just be sure you receive a byline for your efforts. Otherwise, this will be a waste of your time. Never lose sight of the fact that you are writing online content in order to increase awareness about you and your company.

eBook writing is another fantastic way to market yourself. If you think you don't have enough information to fill a book, think again. Your eBook doesn't have to be the length of an average novel. Keep it simple and concise, yet include lots of beneficial information for your readers and that will be enough to drive readers to your company website. Going back to the house sitting business, writing an eBook about homeowner safety and security would be an excellent complement to your business. Making your eBook available via your website as a freebie is a great incentive for potential customers. This will make them want to find out more about you. Do this by including your contact information and pertinent links (you can easily add links to an eBook) at the conclusion so readers can conveniently visit your website straight from your eBook.

Discounts and Coupons

Discounts and coupons are additional proven marketing tactics. Used wisely, coupons and discounts have the potential to entice consumers and turn them from window shoppers to actual customers. You won't get rich by offering coupons to consumers. In fact, be prepared to lose a little bit - after all that's the meaning of a *discount*. However, your true goal when offering coupons and discounts is building *brand awareness*. You're trying to get people to at least *try* your product or service. Once you've accomplished that, you can concentrate on *up-selling* (persuading customers to purchase additional products) and turning new customers into repeat customers.

Successful coupon campaigns should:

- Include expiration dates (creates a sense of urgency)

128

- Contain certain limitations (e.g. no nights and weekends, one per customer, one-time use)
- Include an identifying code to let you know where customers found your coupon (this helps track ROI)
- Serve to move excess inventory or under-used services
- Be used sparingly

You can easily create your own eye-catching coupons with minimal graphic design skills and simple software. These are basically photos with type. This can be accomplished with PowerPoint or even Word. Once you're satisfied with how your coupon looks you can save it as a picture file, ready to be inserted into flyers and other printed matter.

Many businesses now swear by coupon codes. These are used at *checkout*, so they are highly beneficial for online businesses. It's advised to use different coupon codes on different materials and websites. This enables you to track your ROI easily. Increase coupon incentives on sites that do well and do away with those that aren't performing the way you'd like.

You could also trade *likes* and *follows* for discounts. Many businesses are doing this now: *Like us on Facebook and follow us on Twitter to receive a discount* is a phrase commonly seen on business websites.

Contests and Giveaways

People love getting free things - whether they really need them or not. Contests and giveaways can be effective marketing tools if done right. You should decide upfront what it is you're trying to accomplish with a giveaway. Are you simply attempting to entice consumers to sample your product or service? Do you need to build your mailing list? Are your Facebook likes less than stellar and you want to increase your numbers? Maybe you'd like to drive more traffic to your website. Answering these questions before beginning a promotional giveaway will ensure its success.

Whether you sponsor an in-person or online giveaway, you must be certain to adhere to all federal, state and local laws, rules and regulations. These have been put into place to protect consumers from unfair and deceptive advertising practices. For example, you cannot give away "free products", yet require consumers to purchase something in order to enter. Contest rules and regulations vary by state, so be sure to check with your local Consumer Protection Agency to verify the rules according to your locality.

Rafflecopter makes running an online contest practically foolproof. They even randomly pick the winner at the end of the contest. However, if your contest is designed to increase Facebook *likes* or website or Twitter followers you must verify this yourself. Unfortunately, many people enter contests, but do not complete this all-important step. Verifying that entrants have indeed followed or liked your company will eliminate fraudulent entries.

Be creative when choosing prizes. Your own products or services are natural choices. Consider several prizes - a few small trinkets and one large grand prize. Gift baskets are ideal contest prizes. However, if you decide to sponsor an online giveaway, remember that you'll be mailing prizes. Keeping these items small will greatly cut down on your mailing expenses.

Customer Loyalty Programs and Incentives

Many major corporations and companies offer loyalty programs and other incentives in order to entice and retain customers. In fact, it's estimated that 65% of marketers use this marketing tactic. The simplest way to do this is by implementing a point system. You probably have a card or two in your wallet at this moment. You know the kind - a salesperson punches a spot on the card each time you make a purchase. After a predetermined amount of punches, you receive a freebie. These work because they keep customers returning for more until they receive the payoff - a free product or service. According to a recent marketing study, it costs companies 5 to 10 times more to acquire a new customer than it does to sell to an existing one.

Cost is minimal with this marketing option. In fact, if you're handing out business cards (as you should be) you can simply use these. Choose a distinctive paper punch for this purpose to deter cheaters (sorry, it happens). Craft stores sell tons of paper punch options.

Another option would be the VIP treatment. Customers pay an upfront fee and then receive special benefits from that point on. Amazon Prime is a great example of this marketing technique. Consumers pay just under $80 per year and receive unlimited free shipping and other buying incentives. If you knew you could get just about anything from one website, have it shipped right to your front door and not pay a cent for shipping would you pass that up? Probably not. So you see this idea works. You may not be operating a business on the same level as Amazon, but you can certainly use your marketing creativity to come up with a similar idea.

You could also consider teaming up with another small business to create customer incentives to benefit you both. For example, if you operate a pet sitting business you could collaborate with a local dog groomer to offer clients a free dog shampoo after every fifth pet sitting appointment.

Many consumers love playing games. You could design a loyalty program that incorporates a game. Think of McDonalds' Monopoly Game and you get the idea. It certainly doesn't need to be on as grand a scale as that. You could keep it simple by having customers choose a piece of paper from a jar. Each piece of paper either has a prize written on it or a "try again next time". Or, instead, have customers write their name and contact info on a piece of paper, place it in a box and choose winners on a designated date. This has the added benefit of acquiring important information about your customers to be used in future mailings (with their permission of course - add a permission check box for this purpose). The name game is another favorite of consumers. Playing *name the next product* engages customers and gives them a say in a small aspect of your business.

Keeping existing customers interested and connected is the key with incentive and loyalty programs. Be creative with these ideas and gear them towards your particular industry. You'll keep your customers happy for many years to come. Just be sure to keep track of your efforts to ensure that a particular program is working for you.

Stay in Touch with Existing Customers

Christmas cards and even birthday cards are excellent ways to stay in touch with your customers. Personally, I'm always impressed when I receive a greeting card from a company. I'm much more likely to bring my repeat business to a company that goes this extra step.

Refer to your mailing lists and customer contact information. Include a handwritten note and salutation whenever possible. To cut down on postage you could even mail attractive postcards. If your business sells products or centers around photography, artwork or poetry you should consider displaying any of these on the front of your post card or greeting card. Add a holiday touch - your pet donning reindeer antlers makes an adorable pet sitting card. Vistaprint is a great online printing company that specializes in a huge variety of promotional items. They often run money-saving specials throughout the year, so be sure to sign up for their mailing list.

Don't use your greeting cards as sales tactics. This marketing technique is designed solely to stay in touch with customers and let them know you appreciate their business. Your customers will be much more impressed that you're reaching out to them without trying to sell them something.

In Conclusion

Marketing is an ongoing process for business owners. This is definitely not an aspect of your business to ignore. Consistently operating as a positive presence online and within your local community will surely benefit your business. A well-planned, professionally orchestrated marketing plan will position your business above any others like it.

You Can Do This!

We've reached the end of this book. If you take away anything from reading these words, I hope that it's this:

- You can do this!
- Anyone can start a home based business
- You don't need to be rich to start a business
- Think outside the box and find your niche
- There IS a market for your products and/or service
- You're about to work harder than you've ever worked in your life....but...
- It's all worth it!

Get in Touch with Me

I would love to hear your success stories. You might even make it into my next book. That's FREE marketing for you and your business! Please contact me via email at info@thewritewords4you.com or via one of my websites:

The Write Words 4 You
eBook Review Gal
DIY Mom Online

Lastly, if you've found this book, and my previous book, *How To Write, Publish and Market Your eBook*, valuable, I would greatly appreciate it if you'd leave a positive review on Amazon and Goodreads. Writers live for positive reviews and I hope yours will be one of them. Doing so helps us all. Thanks so much.

I wish you much success and happiness in everything you do!

Sincerely,

Susan Elizabeth Barton